PRAY
for
ME

PRAY
for
ME

FINDING FAITH IN A CRISIS

RICK HAMLIN

New York   Nashville

FaithWords
Hachette Book Group
1290 Avenue of the Americas, New York, NY 10104
faithwords.com
twitter.com/faithwords

First edition: September 2017

FaithWords is a division of Hachette Book Group, Inc. The FaithWords
name and logo are trademarks of Hachette Book Group, Inc.

The publisher is not responsible for websites (or their content)
that are not owned by the publisher.

The Hachette Speakers Bureau provides a wide range of
authors for speaking events. To find out more, go to
www.hachettespeakersbureau.com or call (866) 376-6591.

Library of Congress Cataloging-in-Publication Data
Names: Hamlin, Rick, author.
Title: Pray for me : finding faith in a crisis / Rick Hamlin.
Description: first [edition]. | New York : Faith Words, 2017.
Identifiers: LCCN 2017016498| ISBN 9781478921646 (hardcover) | ISBN
9781478921639 (ebook)
Subjects: LCSH: Sick—Religious life. | Prayer—Christianity.
Classification: LCC BV4910 .H363 2017 | DDC 265/.8—dc23
LC record available at https://lccn.loc.gov/2017016498

ISBNs: 978-1-4789-2164-6 (hardcover), 978-1-4789-2163-9 (ebook)

Printed in the United States of America

LSC-C

10 9 8 7 6 5 4 3 2 1

For all of you who prayed—more people than I can count, some whose names I don't even know—I am grateful.

For perfect hope is achieved on the brink of despair when, instead of falling over the edge, we find ourselves walking on the air.

—THOMAS MERTON

CONTENTS

PROLOGUE

It's not what you do, it's what God does. It's not how hard you try, it's how willing you are not to try. It's not all about believing when believing comes hard. It's all about trusting that what little faith you bring to the table is enough, more than enough, the mustard seed of a banquet (and I don't even like mustard).

You're not very good at this, as you tell yourself and others. You sit there on the sofa in the early morning with your eyes closed, your legs crossed, yearning for the divine, and you immediately think of all the things you need to get done that day, the meeting that's supposed to happen, the e-mails you must send, the person you should talk to, the seminar you forgot to put on the calendar. That reminds you of the person you said you would get together with whom you haven't gotten together with just yet, and you want to be perceived as a person of your word, so you feel you should get in touch instead of just letting it go.

You've only been there on that sofa for less than a minute, the sun barely glimpsed over the horizon, and you're already off to the races, the superego riding its mangy horse, hurtling down a well-traveled track, tossing up dust and mud. You think of the check you need to write, a bill you haven't paid; you mentally compute the money in your account, trying to figure out if you can cover it or let it slide. And while you're at it, you wonder how much you've managed to squirrel away in your retirement account and really how much you could take out annually if this stock market continues on its wild roller-coaster ride. Maybe if you were a better money manager you would feel more secure.

Even though this time, this dedicated time, is not about being secure financially; it's a moment you've promised yourself to look to higher things, to connect with a higher power. Why are you wasting it worrying about money and the mortgage and your 401(k)? Do you think Jesus really cares about the S&P or the Dow Jones any more than he cares about people who have too little to even invest in a retirement fund?

You don't want to be this way. You wish you could be like the widow with her mighty mite, putting it in the offering plate, hoping not to be noticed, giving all she has out of love and belief.

The only thing you share with her is an abiding humility. You would be as glad not to be noticed in any Heavenly Competition for Radical Holiness. You wouldn't want anyone to think you are bragging, because you have very little to brag about. Just because you said you write about prayer—to that person at the dinner party who asked you what kind of things you wrote—you wouldn't want her or anyone else to think you're above the fray. It's not like you don't suffer from the same worries as the rest of us or nurture the same envies or have moments you'd rather not mention of woe-begotten shame.

The irony is not lost on you that to be someone who says they write about prayer is to put yourself in an attention-getting realm with holy know-it-all status that is contrary to all that prayer is and does. You don't generally go for people who apologize for who they are before they tell you who they are; their humility is to be as little trusted as the correspondent who signs off, "Humbly yours." If you call attention to your humility, how humble can you really be?

You have your doubts about how prayer works, although God forbid you should waste your time identifying them, raising them to an exalted level far beyond their status or worth, because what you really have is belief, and that's what you want to share more than anything else. It was the gift given to you, the pearl beyond price that merits selling all you have and all you possess and it only increases in value as you give it away. It is the most important thing about you. It is your treasure and the source of all you treasure. Something will happen when you're sitting on that couch. In that twenty minutes there will be a glimmer (or there won't) of something far beyond you, a rent in the fabric, a piercing through the veil, an instant of calm, a sign of reassurance, a signal of connection, a peace that passes all understanding, a breath of fresh air, a touch across the cheek, an awakening of the heart, a sigh, a sensation.

Or, as I say, it won't be there. You're not there for that. It's a bonus, a fringe benefit, as a woman I worked with once said, describing the fur coat she wore, a gift from her husband. I question the merit of surveys on prayer's effectiveness in combating a plethora of complaints, from high blood pressure to depression to heart disease—and hey, I've known all three. How nice, I think, that someone can find something that's quantifiable about prayer. How great for the what's-in-it-for-me seeker. How illuminating for the science section of the newspaper. But it would be like getting married because you're told that married people live longer, happier, healthier lives than unmarried people, and you feel that you should acquire for yourself the same benefits. What about love? What about heedless passion? What about unbridled fun? (You're hearing from a man who loves being married.)

I smile when I pray. At least it feels like I do. My body smiles. I don't hold up a mirror to see and I've never had myself photographed praying, although a young colleague of mine wants to do it for a series of portraits of people in prayer. "I'm not sure I can pray if I know someone is taking pictures of me," I said. Once a *New York Times* photographer wanted to do that, take a picture of me praying on the New York City subway because I like to pray on the subway train. I told the man that he could photograph me reading psalms from my little pocket Bible—no problem—but he couldn't take a picture of me praying there. It would be phony, a charade, like simulated sex in a Hollywood movie. My eyes closed, my head bowed, I'd be listening to the click of the shutter, not God.

I read of a study once—talk about scientific studies—about the benefits of stretching before and/or after vigorous exercise. The researcher was trying to find out if those who stretched suffered from fewer running injuries than those who didn't. As I remember, the study was inconclusive. You couldn't prove anything. The message to me: You stretch because it increases your range of motion. It feels good.

Prayer feels good. You're getting in touch with a larger part of yourself. You're putting things into perspective. You're reaching out for the divine. You're listening to yourself—yes, all those piddling anxieties and worries, and the not-so-piddling ones, that you're going to drop into the lap of the Most Holy and leave them behind as much as is possible or at least until you sit on the sofa again, or the subway or the chair in your office or in your kitchen beneath the ticking clock or in the pew in the empty church or in the folding chair in the twelve-step meeting. This is your holy place, your stretching time.

You're not there to get the great idea for your next novel or what to say at the meeting you'll lead on Thursday or the PowerPoint presentation you have to make. You're not even there to get some clever insight into the spiritual life. The point of prayer is not to watch yourself praying. You're not going to leap off the pillow to rush into the spiritual growth seminar, waving your hand, dying to be called on, saying, "The most amazing thing happened to me when I was praying this morning." OK, you might just do that, but don't plan on it. Don't listen to what you're thinking about the divine. Just listen.

Amazing things will happen. Indeed the great idea for the novel and a whole series of novels or screenplays might come to you. The brainstorm that you've been waiting for will surely descend; the dedicated silence of your prayer session could be a spawning ground for a host of fertile notions, no doubt about it, but you don't need to make huge demands on prayer. Let it deliver what it has to offer, and what it has to offer is itself.

The farmer tills the soil, plants the seed, waters it or waits for the rain to fall. The farmer works hard, but the wondrous thing that happens isn't anything he could do on his own. A tendril pushes up through the ground, the sun shines on it, the rain falls, leaves burst out, branches grow, the stalk rises, blossoms spring forth and fall, fruit fills their place, pulling nutrients from the sky and soil, until the glorious day of the harvest comes, baskets and bins filled to the brim. The miracle is nothing the farmer did; it was done for him.

Put yourself in a place and space where wonders are done for you, where better things will befall you than you would dare ask for, where love prospers and hope flourishes and goodness prevails, where worries about the future are few because the day itself is a source of joy.

CHAPTER ONE

The ER

Here's a leg on my journey of prayer that I need to put down, a time of the worst and the best all at once, an episode worth analyzing, although I dread doing it. I often write to get rid of fears or at least to shrink them into manageable size. There on paper they won't haunt me. They are simply words on a page. Once I asked a best-selling author, "Do you ever pray?" "When I write I pray," he said. I thought I understood what he meant. Anything that requires that level of trust as you gaze into the unknown is prayer. You can't go forward without it.

When I think about writing this, I start talking myself out of it: Don't write about that medical crisis. Don't go there. Who wants to know that you almost died? You're alive now, so it's ancient history. You don't want to relive it anyway. It's over, done with. Why wrestle with it? Why do you feel you must give it some meaning on the page? That's so tiresome. You're still processing it anyway. Let it rest. Give it another ten or twenty years. (Twenty years? Geez, I don't even know if I'll be around in twenty years.) Your readers don't know you all that well. Most of them don't know you at all. How is this going to help them?

Would that I could say like Jesus, "Satan, get behind me," because the dark passages of our lives, when shared, can become healing passages of our lives, for us and for others. I will tell it straight up, and you can decide yourself if it's one long organ recital, as in "Can you top this medical disaster story?" or if it was indeed a winding path of prayer. Forgive me for going into clinical details.

It began two years ago—or at least this part of the story began—with a boil on the back of my leg. It looked like some sort of ingrown hair. (Nice.) "That's looking pretty ugly," my wife, Carol, said, "you should go get that checked out." This being the Saturday of Labor Day weekend, the only place I could think of that would be open was the urgent care facility on 165th Street, around the corner from the Art Deco remains of the Audubon Ballroom (where Malcolm X was shot). The urgent-care place is affiliated with and across the street from the sprawling New York–Presbyterian/Columbia University Medical Center, where all my doctors work. If I could go anywhere, I wanted to be in a spot where they could access my medical records at the click of a computer key.

We live about fifteen minutes away. I jogged down Broadway, past bodegas and Laundromats, a parking garage, and an Irish pub, people pushing strollers and shopping carts. I signed in. Didn't have to wait long. A young doctor checked me out, said that yes, it looked infected, and prescribed two antibiotics. I picked up the pills at Hilltop Pharmacy near our house and started taking them that day. I felt pretty good the rest of the weekend, and the boil looked like it was shrinking.

On Sunday we went to church and that afternoon I

visited a homebound ninety-four-year-old parishioner, Wesley, who'd served with the Tuskegee Airmen during World War II. He was also a superb musician. We sang, as always, a few hymns together—he harmonized from his hospital bed. Too weak to sit up, he could still hold the baritone line. I headed home. Carol and I watched TV that night, an episode of *Broadchurch*, a creepy British mystery series. The next day, Labor Day, I ran some errands, did the laundry, went for a run, washed some windows, vacuumed. So much for a laborless holiday.

On Tuesday I went to work but found myself getting really chilly in the air-conditioned office. I just couldn't get myself warm. Wishing I'd brought a sweater, I wrapped my hands around a mug of tea. "Isn't it cold in here?" I asked my colleagues. "Aren't you freezing?" They humored me but nobody readily agreed. "You probably have a fever," I told myself, gritting my teeth to keep them from chattering, bouncing my legs at my desk to get them warm. Even so, I had no intention of heading home early. There was work to do, five days of it that had to be crammed into a four-day workweek. I'm an editor at *Guideposts* magazine and just because the world took off for Labor Day didn't mean that our deadlines disappeared. In some faintly puritanical stance, I hesitated about taking an ibuprofen because it seemed like doing that would simply mask the fever rather than make it go away.

I left work at the usual hour, shivering on the subway ride home, ate dinner, took my temperature, finally—yes,

I had a fever—and went to bed. Carol's medical advice has always been to give in to whatever you've got sooner rather than later, because you'll get rid of it sooner rather than later. Don't soldier on. Go to bed immediately, take a sick day. Not that I always follow this good advice, but I did then.

I called in sick on Wednesday, the fever not diminishing despite the ibuprofen I was now popping every four hours. I went back to the urgent-care place. They said, "Keep taking the antibiotics." On Thursday I got an appointment with my internist, whose office is in the hospital complex. I like Seth a lot. He's warm, caring, wise, and wry. He's always overbooked, but it's never stopped him from giving his full attention to his patients or insisting, as he once did at the end of a session, on showing me a funny video clip on his computer that I watched over his shoulder while his ever-patient assistants were rolling their eyes and pointing to the clock. I try not to call him Seth but Doctor because I want him to know I respect him and esteem him, but I think of him as Seth.

"It's freezing in here," I said to his assistant when I checked in. The fever speaking.

"Sit in the waiting room," she said. "It's warm in there. The air conditioner isn't working."

"Give him my sweatshirt," Seth called from his office.

They gave me a big gray sweatshirt with NEW YORK–PRESBYTERIAN written on it in red, some swag from a medical conference, I figured. I took a selfie, the coddled patient, and texted it to Carol: "Look what Seth loaned me."

When Seth finally examined me, he listened to my lungs, switched me off one of the antibiotics, had me do some blood tests, and said I might have pneumonia. He sent me to the lab to get a chest X-ray, but all I really wanted to do was get home, get warm, and get in bed. Plenty of rest was the order of the day. He'd let me know if the blood tests showed anything.

"What shall I do with the sweatshirt?" I asked.

"Keep it," he said.

I nursed myself at home on Friday, piling blankets on top of blankets, sipping mugs of tea and broth, even in the warm September weather, and taking these big ibuprofen horse pills. But the fever only got worse. On Saturday morning it spiked at 104.2, with no sign of diminishing. "I should go to the ER," I said to Carol. It was around 11:00 a.m.

"I'm coming with you," she said. "We'll take a cab."

You know it's bad when a tightwad and public transportation junkie like me makes no objections to taking a cab, instead of a bus, the fifteen blocks to the hospital.

We got out at the wrong corner and had to walk half a block more—it felt like half a mile—to the entrance of the emergency room. I expected the usual long wait, like trying to flag down a salesperson at Macy's the week before Christmas, but we sat in the anteroom for less than fifteen minutes before I was admitted. I guess they could tell I was pretty bad off, every breath becoming a struggle, my body trembling to stay warm.

Half aware, half in a daze, I felt myself slipping down

mortality's rabbit hole with no desire to reach out to the divine.

How can I explain this? How can I show it? It's at the crux of what I struggle to understand about prayer and the life of the spirit. When my body goes, my faith goes too, and long-practiced spiritual habits hardly count. I remembered this from open-heart surgery. When I'm really sick—and I was really sick then, sicker than I'd ever been—my spirit diminishes. The world becomes smaller, and all my internal anguish takes over. I am not a holy person at all but some poor soul caught in a trap. I want to be able to cry out to God but I can't. I monitor the downward spiral I'm being sucked into, and find no means of salvation. I've read about the saints who found pain and suffering a means for drawing closer to the Lord of sorrows, the one who died on a cross for us. But physical suffering isolates me from such love and solace. I am consumed with myself and forget about my Maker. When I think about dying, this is what worries me most. That I would become such a stranger to myself. Am I just a sunshine patriot and no winter soldier? Is not my faith bigger than this?

Did I think I was dying? Not then. My brain sank into a fog. The techs and nurses put me on oxygen and an IV drip. We were lodged in a cubicle with curtains at the sides, a pod with other patients across from me and Carol in a chair next to me. Everything was illuminated with bright lights whether we were awake or asleep. They hustled me off on a gurney or in a wheelchair for an echocardiogram—I think—and a lung X-ray. They took my temperature and drew blood. The nurses and doctors came and went. I dozed and stared and wondered how long I would have to stay in the ER. Surely they would admit me into the hospital. Maybe they would send me home. What time was it? Couldn't Carol go home? Much of this is fuzzy to me, but then there were moments I was acutely aware of.

I remember when the aides were decking me out in a gown and those non-slippery socks they give you in hospitals. "Not the yellow ones," one woman said to another. "Those are only for the violent ones." I looked at the multi-tattooed patient across from me, a kid who appeared to be strung out on a drug overdose, rattled and shaking. He had yellow socks. A violent one?

The woman next to me was ninety-nine years old—I heard her say that—and I hoped for her sake she could go home and die in her bed rather than this place. She was in a plain gown with brown socks. The woman across from us, in her mere seventies I supposed, resented being told that she was being sent to the hospital's uptown outpost. "I want to stay right here. I don't want to go to the Allen Pavilion," she said, as though she were being asked to shop at a suburban branch of Saks when she was at the Fifth Avenue store.

I must have been seen by more than one doctor, but the only one I remember was a young one with blondish-brown hair, a three-day beard, and a bad bedside manner. He talked to the nurse or Carol about what grave trouble I was in, as though I were too far gone to understand his words, like talking about a deaf person in front of them. I recall him saying my condition was critical, and I realized the adjective had a very specific meaning here, like when they say on the news, "The victim was taken to the hospital and remains in critical condition."

He took my blood pressure. "Ninety over fifty," he said.

"Wow, that's pretty good," I thought to myself. "I've been trying to get it down." Like an anorexic on death-watch, congratulating herself for being a skeletal eighty-nine pounds.

The endless afternoon and evening wore on. Carol must have gone out to get some food. I don't remember eating, myself. Our twenty-five-year-old son, Timothy, was living with us at the time—and soon to leave on a ten-month mission trip to South Africa. Carol let him know where we were. He texted or called from Brooklyn, where he was at a party with his girlfriend. "Should I come by the hospital?" he asked. "You don't need to," Carol texted back. He knew her and me better than that and showed up at the ER after midnight. I remember him being there. I remember him talking to Carol and me. And then he left.

At 2:00 a.m. they finally admitted me.

I was taken to the step-down unit of the ICU on the sixth floor. They pushed me in a wheelchair on the sky-bridge across Fort Washington Avenue. I'd seen it from below many times but had never been on it. It was the middle of the night and the corridor was lit up like the

inside of a refrigerator. I could see the lights of the hospital
out the windows, and it seemed as enchanted as the Emer-
ald City. I think of a friend's mother who, when given last
rites, exclaimed in wonder, "I've never done this before!"
Another friend tells the story of his ailing ninety-three-
year-old mother being airlifted off of Martha's Vineyard
to get emergency medical care, her last flight on earth,
and all she could say about it was, "That was the first time
I've ever been on a helicopter!"

Perhaps that's how the spirit speaks when you're not
conscious of making any prayer and feel incapable of it.
You can still see things to marvel at. I wanted to turn to
the aide pushing my wheelchair and tell him, "Gosh, I've
never been on this bridge before." But the mask blowing
oxygen into my lungs didn't allow for talking.

On the other side of the bridge, in the step-down unit,
I kissed Carol good-bye or, more likely, she kissed me
because of my oxygen mask. "Go home. Get some sleep," I
wanted to say, although I couldn't really speak.

The next morning, Sunday, September 13, Carol sent
the first of her mass e-mails:

Dear ones, forgive the mass e-mail but this is the
easy way to start this news moving around. Please
feel free to forward this e-mail—I started with a bare-
bones approach.

Rick has had pneumonia since Thursday and
took a turn for the worse yesterday. We went to the

emergency room at Columbia-Presbyterian, and at length he was admitted to a step-down unit—a slightly tamer version of the ICU. He is getting great care.

He is very sick. Sepsis was one diagnosis, along with pneumonia, but he was having trouble getting oxygen. When I left him a few hours ago he had on a device that blows oxygen into his lungs.

That's all I can tell you now, but I will keep you apprised, probably via a blast e-mail. Add names if you like.

He doesn't have a phone at his bed (retro!) but he will have access to his cell. Right now he's so sick I don't dare leave it there with him. Ditto computer. Tim is here and we will probably tag team for the next few days.

No visits or phone calls for now but I will pass along messages. E-mails to me might be best—I can print them out and take them to him.

I know you want to know what you can do. If you are praying people, do that. Otherwise, keep us in your thoughts.

Lots of love to you all.

Carol

P.S.: I am not really taking calls either but I am texting madly. Always assuming I remember to charge my phone!

CHAPTER TWO

Hospital, Day 1

When Timothy was four he broke his femur in a tricycle accident at nursery school. In those pre–cell phone days, Carol called work and left me an urgent message. I was at a dentist appointment and when I walked into the office the receptionist let me know Carol was trying to reach me. I listened to a few messages on my office phone, one telling me about the accident, one telling me how she had picked up William, our older son, from school, one telling me where she had taken Tim for an X-ray, one telling me where I should meet her and the boys.

I rushed uptown to an unfamiliar hospital building near Columbus Circle, not Columbia-Presbyterian, where both boys had been born. I struggled to find them, bouncing around from floor to floor, going up and down in the elevator. Finally I spoke to a person who told me Carol had taken Timothy down to the Hospital for Joint Diseases on East Seventeenth Street. I raced back downtown and at the hospital went up to what I thought was pediatrics. I got off the elevator to hear a doctor in green scrubs say to another doctor, "It's the worst break I've ever seen in a kid. Right through his femur. They said it was a tricycle-riding accident at nursery school, but it's hard to imagine any kid could get hurt that bad by a tricycle."

Some conversations you don't want to overhear.

I asked the doctors where I could find my son, the patient. I was sent back downstairs. Finally I found Carol and seven-year-old William sitting next to Tim in a crib with bars around it like a prison cell. He was lying on his back, his broken leg wrapped in bandages and held up in a swing-like device. He would have to be like that for twenty-six days, in traction. "It's a little like being trapped on an airplane with a toddler for twenty-six days," his babysitter Sharon later observed.

Carol was doing a good job of acting calm in the storm, wearing her best Florence Nightingale face—Nurse Barbie in action—but she was clearly frazzled. "I'll spend the night here with Tim," I said. "We'll be OK." We would have to alternate roles, one parent with the child at home, the other in the hospital with Tim.

That night Tim and I were in a double room, where the kid on the other side of the curtain was crying and his parents were watching a shoot-'em-up movie on TV, the sound blasting through the curtain. I sat in a chair that could be turned into a bed and tried to coax Tim to go to sleep. He and I dozed, on and off, but he woke up several times in the night, the TV still blaring on the other side of the room, the soundtrack in a minor key. I remember Tim grabbing the bars of his crib and clutching them like some prisoner. "Daddy," he said, "we're stuck."

"Yes, Tim-o," I said. "We're stuck."

That was how I felt now in my hospital room, stuck. I

had a mask delivering oxygen to me, monitors connected to my heart, an IV drip filling me with pints of fluid. I couldn't go anywhere even if I wanted to. I was still feverish and whenever the fever spiked, I felt short of breath. I could barely talk. The first of many doctors began their procession by my bedside. Columbia-Presbyterian is a teaching hospital, and that meant an extensive cast of characters: residents, interns, physicians, plus the nurses, techs, and aides. This was the new routine.

That morning, like every morning, a beefy guy who looked like a truck driver came in with a big machine to give me a chest X-ray. I assumed the equipment was heavy. Three times a day a sweet-faced woman brought in a tray with breakfast, lunch, or dinner. The food was not very good, but I wanted to eat it because she was lovely and I didn't want to disappoint her, her voice musical with the inflection of some Caribbean island.

Then there were the doctors, interns, and residents. They asked the same questions over and over again. "Have you traveled lately?"

"We were in Southern California visiting my family in July."

"Have you been overseas?"

"We went to Budapest and Vienna in June." This was a dream trip that our sons gave us for Christmas, our anniversary, and our sixtieth birthdays combined, twenty-eight-year-old William cashing in thousands of frequent-flier miles he had garnered from business trips.

"Any other trips? Anything exotic?"

"We went to Kenya about three years ago." We have friends who have been working for several years on a water project in a small village outside Nairobi, building a well, which we got to see. We also took a safari to far-flung places.

"Do you have any pet birds?"

"No." We have a very large, very lazy cat, Fred, named for Frederick Douglass because he was rescued from the A-train platform in Harlem, near Frederick Douglass Boulevard. He's also hirsute like Douglass, with a combination of black, gray, and white hair.

"Have you ever worked in a shipyard?"

"No."

"Have you worked on a ship?"

"No," I said to this, although a good friend with whom I'd performed in a half-dozen amateur Gilbert and Sullivan productions later insisted I should have said, "I've served on the *H.M.S. Pinafore*."

I wanted to be helpful. I wanted to give them answers that would lead to a diagnosis, but it was hard to keep my head clear and to speak when I was struggling for breath. The mask went over my nose so I could still get oxygen and speak but it made me claustrophobic.

In between the diagnostic Q and A's I slept fitfully. You never sleep well in a hospital, and yet sleep is what you long for. There are too many interruptions, too much noise, too much discomfort, too much light.

It was Sunday, my first day. Carol appeared after church. "Everyone asked about you," she said. Word had spread. She'd put my name on the prayer list and maybe hers too. She is usually loath to admit to needing help—aren't we all?—but she unloaded to the first person she saw at church, someone who'd shown up early for the service, not even a close friend. Is there ever a time when you need church more? Complete strangers are the closest intimates when you worship together week after week. They know you, you know them, you will be with them in times of need, they will be with you. You have known their prayers.

After lunch Kate, our rector, appeared. Two services in the morning and another service in the evening, not to mention coffee hours, forums, and meetings, but she managed to come.

I think of the son of a friend who had his first day of high school on 9/11 at a school not far from the World Trade Center. The students were sent home after the second plane crashed into the second tower. There was no public transportation, so they just kept walking north, the conflagration behind them. The minute the disaster happened the boy's father, our friend, headed for the school, determined to find his son. They met on the West Side Highway, father and son, one walking south, one walking north. "I knew you'd come," the boy said to his dad.

I knew you'd come. That's what I wanted to say to Kate. Not that there was any mystery about where she'd find me, but she was the connection to my church, to all those people who looked out for me as I looked out for them. She glanced at me in her clerical collar, her worried face telling me exactly how bad I looked. She'd brought her black-leather-bound *Book of Common Prayer* and was ready to pray.

Between halting breaths of air I told her, "I'm in despair. That's what I need...hope. Despair is the enemy."

I was at rock bottom, no shred of optimism left in me, no faith. This was far worse than the breaths I couldn't take or the oxygen that didn't seem to saturate me or the fever that sent my body into chills or my inability to complete a sentence without wheezing or the doctors' mystified stares and their inability to come up with a diagnosis. I had no hope. I remembered a college classmate who had a malignant brain tumor in his early forties and had countless miniseizures a day. "I have to hold on to hope," he said to me, a short seizure interrupting our conversation, his eyes glazing over for a few seconds. "As long as I have hope, I'm OK." I thought of my aunt, a lifelong smoker, dying of lung cancer at sixty-three. There she was coughing up a storm, then taking a drag on a cigarette, while we pretended she was going to get through this. "I have to hope," she said.

That morning, before church let out, before Kate showed up, I remember thinking, "You're at the bottom, Rick. You're sicker than you've ever been before. You can't get any lower than this."

Then I had an even scarier thought: in a hospital, they dropped the bottom down even lower than where I already was. They would put patients in induced comas or give them a tracheotomy or put them on ventilators or feed them through tubes in their stomachs. They could make despair last for days or weeks or months by simply keeping you alive. What would be the point?

Here I was, a so-called person of faith, a man with a spiritual practice, and I was drowning in despair, overwhelmed with it, benumbed. They could blow oxygen into my lungs all they liked but what I yearned for was the breath of the Spirit. The things I normally did, closing my eyes to meditate, wiping my mind of all its anxieties and worries—putting on the mind of Christ, if you will—taking in a deep breath, listening to God by becoming very still, were impossible. Maybe if I'd had my Kindle with me, with its Bible that I read on the subway to work, highlighting favorite passages...but it was still at home, and even if I'd had it, I couldn't have concentrated. It would have been like searching for meaning in the classified ads.

I needed Kate to be there. I needed to vent, revealing my struggle. She listened, she prayed. Oh, how grateful I was for her prayers, although I didn't feel any relief. Not then. Not yet.

She left. More doctors came and went. Food trays came, and I tried to eat but had no appetite—not that the beef Stroganoff or the chicken cutlet or the fruit salad or the chocolate pudding in a plastic cup or the grayish beans and brownish peas were that appetizing. Taking the plastic wrapping off a roll or trying to get the butter out of its metallic wrap was an exercise in occupational therapy. It took all my strength. (I write this here, but I don't think I could eat much of anything yet. Not Sunday. I wasn't well enough.)

The day nurse had appeared after seven that morning, writing her name down in red marker on the white board opposite my bed, erasing the name of the night nurse who had been on duty. I wanted to talk to the nurses and aides and techs, ask them where they were from, where they lived, where they had gone to school, find some way of connecting that wasn't just caregiver/patient. A question or two could take me out of myself and my misery, but conversation between breaths was almost impossible.

"You live...in New Jersey...very far away?"

"Do you...have...children?"

"Where did you...go to...nursing school?"

"Do you...like...being a...nurse?"

They took my blood pressure, my temperature, dispensed pills, took my blood, changed whatever was in the IV drip, adjusted the tubes giving me oxygen, brought me bedpans and took them away. They checked out whatever the machines said, recording the numbers, but not once did I feel they were just looking at the machines above my head. They were looking at me.

"I have to get out of here soon," I thought, absurdly

enough. "I've got a big conference in California to attend in two weeks. I have to be there."

I hated to put Carol through this, hated to drag her away from the repose of a Sunday nap or the Sunday *Times*, or a football game on TV—and it was she who followed the NFL, not me, she who watched the games with the boys. Now she was running interference for me in a drab hospital room. She could ask the doctors questions and understand their answers. She could respond to the litany of their queries: no, we had no wild birds; no, I had never worked in a shipyard; no, we hadn't been to any exotic locale recently; no, I had never served on a ship. I wanted to talk but I was too tired to talk. I wished she could get lost in a good book, but she was too worried for that. And the interruptions were constant. Here we were, two people whose love for each other was greater than words, and there were no words to describe the mess I was in, not even a diagnosis.

Timothy was there that day, and at one point when no one else was in the room, he sat in the chair in the corner and read a psalm in that careful way he reads aloud, not overdramatic, his voice comfortable with each phrase, like he's really talking to you, not reading. I don't remember which psalm he read, I wasn't even sure it really happened, my brain in a fog, my memory faulty, my faith habits nil. If I couldn't manage to read a psalm, had I imagined someone else doing it for me? Was it all a fantasy?

A couple of weeks later I e-mailed him in South Africa.

"That first day I was in the hospital, did you sit by my bed and read a psalm to me?"

"Yes," he replied. He couldn't remember which psalm either.

This is when I picture some underground system like the pneumatic tube network that ran under the streets of Paris, delivering packets of information and documents from one building to another. I can see the pipes racing out in one direction, carrying their disturbing news, urging others to send spiritual sustenance and healing—urgent healing—back my way. I can imagine some wan signal or message, a dim bulb, a faint flickering, coming from me, and a blinding flood of warmth and light returning, people caring and praying and hoping and believing what I couldn't possibly have believed on my own. It's all completely unscientific and unprovable and vague in my *Charlie and the Chocolate Factory* imagining. "Can't you come up with a better metaphor?" I ask myself. Can't you come up with something more gracious and elegant, or at least something that holds together? Why do you see all of this as plumbing?

As soon as I had any sort of voice and could talk, I would call my eighty-nine-year-old mother, who lives out in California. I wanted her to hear my voice from the hospital so that, despite her fears, she could know I lived and spoke and was sentient. Over the phone for a few minutes I hoped to fake good cheer for her, just to make her feel better. Maybe I would fake hope, too, talk myself out of despair.

But I don't think you can talk yourself out of despair. You need something coming back to you, you need something filling you up from the inside, you have to have something big to hold on to, you can't just clutch at air.

I didn't know when Carol sent out her first group e-mail. It might have been from the hospital or during the limited time she had at home, when she wasn't by my bedside. I had no idea who was on her list. The whole idea of putting together a list like that would be daunting even if I was in the best of health.

"I've let everybody know where you are," she said on Sunday. "I told them they can text me or e-mail me back. And you're on the prayer list at church." She promised to read me what people said but if she had done that with every e-mail, she would have wept. Some she eventually printed out. Some she showed me on her laptop. Some I never saw until I was quite well. I was glad she said no phone calls. I wouldn't have been able to handle that. It was hard enough for her to keep track as her e-mails went viral, people sharing them with other people who knew me or knew of me or didn't know me from Adam but somebody had told them to add me to their prayer list and they wanted to let her or me know. I still meet friends of friends who say, "We were praying for you."

The prayers reached for me down in my pit of despair. Think of how your brain can leap and jive and plummet off a cliff to the worries and fears of "what might happen" and "how things can go wrong," or maybe, possibly, with a little help, "how things can go right," and then imagine a mental state where you can't even set your mind into any future-thinking at all because your present feels so dreary, so dark, so sepulchral. You feel too stuck to even be anxious, too rotten to be depressed.

Love was headed my way, if I could only fathom it, an onslaught to do battle with my despair. I was already upheld by Carol's presence, Tim's psalms, the nurses darting in and out, the doctors' concerns, the lovely lady bringing the food trays, hugging Carol and promising to pray, the minister from our church coming to me in the midst of her busiest day. That I even thought "I knew you'd come" was surely a sign of hope when I couldn't recognize it. I wasn't up for visitors or phone calls. "I got the nicest e-mail from...," Carol could say.

September 14, 5:39 p.m.

Forgive me, dear friends, for silence. I got tangled in multiple e-mail chains so some of you are getting double info and some have e-mailed Rick and not heard back and that's the state of play right now. He still doesn't have enough energy to read e-mail so there's a stack of lovely messages in his inbox (I forwarded rather than printing) that will delight him when he can read them. And again, keep up the forwarding. I know I'm missing people.

Not much to report. He's a little stronger today— can sit in the chair for a little while, say a sentence or two. Still getting oxygen, still often very short of breath. Docs are stumped. Keep asking probing questions like, "Have you ever kept birds as pets?"

Just pause and imagine that: the NYC Hamlins with pet birds. Um, no.

But best, this morning, from the pulmonology team, to RICK HAMLIN: "Have you ever worked in a shipyard?" They both looked at him as if they understood what a foolish question it was, but had to ask it anyway.

So obviously we have turned into an episode of "House" and we need to have Hugh Laurie turn up at the door. Which would be kind of cool.

Still believe the care is excellent. Rick is still in step-down and not going anywhere soon, it seems. The extensive monitoring is important. Problem is that they can't treat until they know *what* to treat.

Nothing you guys can do yet. I'm sure a time will come when he gets better and then gets bored and we'll invite you to visit or call, but he's far from that stage for now. Let it be said that he has an angelic temperament and is enduring this with patience. We are literally supported by your concern and your prayers.

Lots of love, Carol

CHAPTER THREE

ICU, Day 2

W hen I came home after spending that first night with four-year-old Tim in traction, I was completely rattled. "I don't know how we're going to do this," I said to Carol. "I can't imagine having to stay with him in that hospital for twenty-six days and nights." I still had to go to the office during the day. Carol worked at home so she had more flexibility than I did. But there was also seven-year-old William at home. Someone had to watch him. How would we take care of the kids and how would we take care of each other? How would any of us get any sleep? At least Will would be off at school, and there was the babysitter, who came in the afternoons.

It was a Friday, Good Friday, so I had the day off from work. But I was expected to sing in choir at the Good Friday service at church that day. I hustled off for rehearsal and the noonday service.

I came home that afternoon to more bad news. William, it seemed, had chicken pox, red splotches all over his skin. He needed to be quarantined for ten days. A bath of milk was supposed to be soothing.

Will lay in bed, reading. I kissed him on his head, the place my father would kiss me, and rejoined Carol in the living room.

Now we had two sick children on our hands, two

parents with not enough hands. How were we going to manage? It was struggle enough to keep all the balls in the air on a good day: work, school, children, shopping. Friday night was my night at the supermarket. I would gather all the empty cans and bottles—five cents a pop—and put them in the fold-up cart, then head up to the pathetically understocked A&P at 187th Street. I cruised the aisles with the list, Cap'n Crunch for Will, frozen waffles for Tim (he liked to eat them just like that, frozen), Progresso beans and Campbell's corn chowder, boxes of mac and cheese, Rice-A-Roni, ramen noodles that were dubbed "Sharon noodles" in our house because they were our babysitter Sharon's favorite.

That was how we managed, divide and conquer, split up the parenting duties and we could get it all done, baths, bed, books, homework, laundry.

Throw one wrench into the works, and life would lurch and plunge. Throw two wrenches into the works, and it would spin out of control. The image that came to me was of being at the edge of a merry-go-round that was cranked up to top speed, and everything would start flying off, including us.

I sat on the futon and held my head in my hands. "I don't see how the center can hold," I said.

"We'll manage," Carol said. "We'll figure it out." She's usually the worrier, unless I become worried and then, alternating roles, she becomes the stronger one, ultracapable, organizing, planning, checking off lists, keeping her worries to herself. Divide and conquer again.

"We'll call Mom." Mom could come out and help. She'd done that when the children were born, devoting a week to us with one morning off to go to the Metropolitan Museum and indulge in art, a pretzel on the steps in the sun her lunch. Could she come out now? Then we'd be three adults for two kids, a better ratio.

First we let the hospital know that Timothy had been exposed to chicken pox.

"He'll need to be quarantined," they said. We'd have to put on masks and gowns when we visited him, we'd have to wash our hands and wear gloves. But, first things first, he'd have to be moved to a private room. That was the one silver lining: he'd be by himself. Easier to sleep at night.

I called Mom. She volunteered before I could ask. She appeared that Easter weekend, with a bottle of California wine for the parents (as though California wine was not available in New York) and Easter baskets for the boys. Tim was princely in his hospital bed, staring at that singing purple dinosaur on TV, his foot permanently aloft. He had adjusted, would adjust. I secretly resented that there was no Easter Bunny to visit him, nobody bringing jelly beans. Wasn't that the sort of thing that happened in children's wards?

Mom took the subway train to the hospital in the morning, the A train to Fourteenth Street, then the L train across town to Third Avenue. She would be with Timothy during the day, while I went to work and Carol was with Will, and then we'd switch around in the evening, one of us parents sleeping in the foldout bed next to Tim, in traction, every night.

Mom was the eternal good sport, good-natured, sunny-tempered. The only thing she really didn't like was the train ride.

"But it's the place I pray," I said. My morning commute on the A train was my prayer time, the rumble of the train on the tracks like some sort of call to worship. I'd read a psalm from my tattered pocket Bible and then close my eyes somewhere around 125th Street, checking out to check in. This time, this place, this connection to keep me going. Some days it was the only thing that made sense.

I bought Carol twenty-six chocolate truffles, so she could mark off the days, her Advent calendar of hope. Our friends came and visited Tim in his princely room, putting on masks and gowns because he had been exposed to chicken pox. Someone gave him a disposable camera, and he took pictures of them from his horizontal point of view—we still have a scrapbook of the results. "I can't believe it," our friends remarked, "two crises all at once. One sick child here, one at home."

What we refrained from saying but still thought was, "Don't these things come in threes?" What shoe would be next to drop? It's a sort of reverse faith, expecting the disaster begotten by a disaster begotten by a disaster, a glass-half-empty mentality, mumbo jumbo, and yet it was there.

The staff at the hospital was lovely. We always promised ourselves that we would go back when Timothy was well so we could thank them for their care.

But we never went back. When something like that is over, you don't want to revisit it at all. You want it to be over, completely over. Done with.

My second night in the ICU step-down unit was the worst. I hardly slept. I was being given oxygen, tubes running into my nose, the monitor ready to beep or scream or whatever it did when my oxygen levels sank to the danger level. Every half hour that night the monitor beeped, waiting for the nurse to come in and check it. All night I was awakened every time I dozed off because I wasn't getting enough oxygen. (Like I said, hospitals are terrible places for sleeping.) Finally I asked the night nurse, "Could you please lower the alarm...so it doesn't keep...waking me up?" Better a good night's sleep than not enough oxygen, better dead than harangued by beeping machines.

"A man who keeps death before his eyes will at all times overcome his cowardice," said one of the Desert Fathers.

But who wants to think about death all the time? Who wants an alarm alerting us to the continual truth, "You will die. You might already be dying. You could be getting close this time"?

I have a very loud heartbeat. I can hear it beating

whenever I am still. In the audience during a concert, sitting before my computer, in a conference room during a meeting, in my bed when I'm waiting to fall asleep, on the sofa when I'm praying, in church when I'm singing (no, my heart rarely beats in time to the music). About the only time I can't hear it is when I'm running or when I'm on the subway, and the rumble of the train on the tracks is loud enough to bury the sound.

There are two ways to think about the sound of the beating heart, one upbeat and one not so cheery. It's a reminder—beat, beat, beat—that "You're still alive. Your heart is functioning. It's pumping blood through your system. You are on God's green earth. Enjoy it." Or the sound of the heart in your ears will say to you, "Your heart will stop someday. It can't always be working so hard, making all this noise. And didn't it just skip a beat? The light goes on and the light goes off. The beat goes on and the beat goes off. You won't hear it someday, because your heart won't be working. When that happens, you won't be."

To be conscious of your beating heart is a double-edged sword, a source of anxiety or a source of comfort. I'm most comfortable when distracted by work or writing or listening or caring or praying so that I don't hear it at all. It feels like the mark of a successful day. The less I hear my heart—the less self-conscious I am of it—the better I will have lived.

Does that sound judgmental?

I would like to think that to live with the knowledge of

death is to see how precious each day is, how it is all that we're given and all that we have on this earth, every hour a chance to give and love until we return to our Maker. "Make each day your masterpiece," said legendary UCLA basketball coach John Wooden. Make each day your Rembrandt, your Van Gogh, your Sistine Chapel ceiling.

But that's so hard to do when you can barely move, can barely breathe.

The doctors came and went that day, all of them looking concerned, checking my vitals (that word *vitals*, an adjective turned into a noun through the addition of one letter). The only one who was a real crepe hanger was an older specialist in rheumatology. She arrived with a younger colleague in tow. The two of them checked me out, staring at the numbers on the monitors. She asked me a few questions and then she sat in the chair next to Carol and said, as though I were too sick to hear the news, "You need to prepare yourself for him to be intubated. He's not getting any better now and he's not getting enough oxygen."

Everyone else was holding out hope of some improvement, or pretending they were. Not she. Maybe she knew something the rest didn't know. Maybe she was the only realist in the bunch and was simply being honest. Whatever. I was appalled, frightened, and angry. "Get out of here!" I wanted to say, fighting the urge to pick something off the lunch tray and throw it at her, the uneaten fruit cocktail, the applesauce—as if I could throw anything.

Not getting any better? What did she know? I usually have undying respect for doctors. Not for her.

The weirdest thing that happened to me that second day in the ICU step-down unit, when I was surely at my worst, was an internal change that didn't register on any monitor. Maybe it occurred before she visited or maybe after—I'm not at all sure which. I can't find the exact time for it. There was no come-to-Jesus moment or bolt of lightning. I didn't suddenly sit up in bed and shout, "Wow!" No, it was more subtle and subterranean, a rising tide pulling me out of my despair, a warm bath that was being made ready for me to submerge in. I could have hardly described it. All I knew was that somehow I was going to get better.

I should put a drumroll of prose in here or write it down in all caps: I KNEW I WAS GOING TO GET BET-TER AND GET OUT OF THE HOSPITAL ALIVE.

Where did this come from? Was it my body telling me something that the doctors couldn't begin to see, my organs sending a message to my brain? Was it just wishful thinking? Was it faith?

"You might have to drag a can of oxygen around for the rest of your born days, Rick," I thought, "but you will get better." Perhaps I would never run again or sing again or give a talk at a retreat, but I would walk out of that hospital on my own two feet, no wheelchair, no special ambulance to take me home.

I didn't tell anyone this news. Didn't want to jinx it. It was too tender and fragile—*I* was too tender and fragile. People would have thought I was under some illusion. The machines were on their side. And anyway, my words could only come haltingly, each phrase punctuated by some deep intake of air, an intake that was never enough. I would try to suck in as much oxygen as possible through those tubes in my nose and breathe it out through my mouth. Every time my temperature rose, the breathing became harder. "More ibuprofen," I said. "I have a fever." They couldn't give it to me fast enough. It was the only thing that helped. I counted the hours between pills. When the fever went down I could breathe—mind you, only with the help of machines.

There was no immediate sign of improvement, nothing the doctors could tell me. Jay, the day nurse, one of my favorites, brought around one of those plastic boxes that you're supposed to blow into to make the balls in it rise and float; the longer you can keep them up, the better. They look like a children's toy and are meant to prevent you from getting pneumonia, keeping your breath flowing. Jay demonstrated how it worked, making the balls inside rise and float effortlessly. It was sort of like watching the strong man at the circus ring the bell on the first try.

"Here, you try," he said.

I blew into it, and the plastic balls hardly budged.

"Can't you do better than that?" he asked. He took it

again and demonstrated. I took it back and blew with all my strength into the tube. Hardly any response.

"Keep trying," he said, and left it on my hospital table.

Carol looked to be at the end of her rope. No amount of sweetness could hide her worry. *Do I look that bad? Yes, that bad.*

And yet, and yet—how often can you write the words "and yet"?—I was going to get better. My body knew it or my spirit knew it and was telling my body this good news. There was no laying on of hands, no visit from a hospital chaplain (in the two weeks I was there I was never once visited by a hospital chaplain). But I knew I was being prayed for. That was clear from the e-mails Carol shared. Nobody prayed aloud in that hospital room except our hardworking rector and our son reading a psalm aloud in the corner. But people were praying.

I've always believed that when you can't pray for yourself, it's other people's prayers that sustain you. They do what you can't do. It was the sort of thing that motivated me to pray for others. Some of the writers I edited started a "Jog and Pray for Rick" campaign on Facebook because they knew I prayed when I ran, and now the prayers were going viral. After all, what do you do when you're desperate? What do you do when you can't do much else, beyond sending flowers or a box from Fresh Direct or fruit from Harry & David or a card or a note? What do you do when you want to make a difference? You pray hard and hope for the best.

Sept. 15, 10:00 p.m.

First, an apology: I know I'm not keeping perfect track of this list. Feel free to forward—and if you get this note AS a forward and want to be on the list, just let me know again.

Second, a request: no long-distance diagnosis or prescribing, please. I am listening to a lot of new information now and I want to focus on the stuff coming from the folks in the white coats.

OK, now the update. Drama in the morning: spike in temperature, funky O2 numbers, threats of move to ICU. Scary. But that resolved and I am now looking at a monitor that reads 100% oxygen saturation through the high-flow machine. (Feel free to let your eyes glaze over on details.) R looks a lot better and they are letting him eat but he has less energy than he did yesterday. Terrible night, monitor beeping the whole time, which may contribute.

Still no diagnosis. Most infections have been ruled out and a rheumatology team is now involved, looking at autoimmune issues.

Care continues fabulous. The cast of characters is huge and attentive and some of them are even charming.

Will arrives Thursday morning very early. He probably just wants to get in on all the fun Tim and I are having here with Rick.

Keep those prayers coming. He's still too sick for visitors or calls, and doesn't really have enough energy to read e-mail, but I have been telling him about your concern.

Lots of love from 6 Garden South, Carol

CHAPTER FOUR

ICU, Day 3

To love is to pray, anything that can take you out of yourself. Timothy recently reminded me of a verse from the first letter of John: "Those who do not love a brother or sister whom they have seen, cannot love God whom they have not seen." Lying in a hospital bed, the world of the unseen feels so close, even when it's many miles away.

It was earthly love that helped me grasp who God was, the hound of heaven racing after me as though I were some rabbit lure, and then coming around to meet me at the end of the race, me half out of breath, the everlasting arms ready to embrace me. God had been there all along. "Our Creator, Redeemer, Lover," the nun said in a benediction at our church, words that might have been of frequent usage for her, but they stunned me with newness. "Creator" and "Redeemer"—I'd heard all that before. But "Lover"? What a delicious shock. Yes, I knew what that was. Lover, like my wife.

Here Carol was, coming and going from my hospital room in the ICU, and I was being reminded of what love can do and will do beyond any power of its own.

That we became a couple and married some thirty years ago still seems like a miracle beyond our choosing. We were in the same class at Princeton, but she had all the patina of the East Coast—a private-school background, a bookish temperament, a sophisticated wit, a preppy wardrobe—and I was a public high-school kid from California in flared pants and tennis shoes, out of my depth. For a long while I felt like an outsider looking in, trying to read the hidden clues. Breathless, I was determined to catch up, but I wouldn't have wanted any of my Princeton classmates to know how hard I worked at it. After all, effortlessness was supposed to count for something.

Secretly I went through *Time* magazine and circled words I didn't know, looking them up so I could use them, praying to God I got the pronunciation right. When any of my classmates wanted to play "You tell me your SAT scores, and I'll tell you mine," I kept my mouth shut. I figured it must have been some accident of the admissions office that let me in. Once, freshman year, playing a game of Dictionary, I picked the word *misogyny*, hoping I could stump my friends, having never heard the word before. "I see what you're doing," said one guy, "trying for a double fake out." "Sure," I said, figuring I could hide my ignorance by pretending I was way ahead of them. Maybe there was some third or fourth definition of "misogyny" that nobody knew.

I'd been pretty confident in high school, with a host of really good friends. We had a good time. ("Nobody should be deliriously happy in high school," Carol says. "It just goes against the grain.") Not that I was cool—I've never been cool—but I found a niche where I could be quirky and popular at the same time, the guy who mimicked Fred Astaire when hypnotized at a school assembly, the tenor crooner in the school production of *Brigadoon*. When I got the welcome packet from Princeton with the mystifying word "matriculation," I felt I was gearing up for the big leagues. My LA-born-and-bred grandmother assured me that people were much more formal "back East." I figured I knew what that meant, putting on a madras jacket like we did when we went to the Music Center for some show put on by the Los Angeles Civic Light Opera.

Dad took me to his favorite haberdasher to get suited up. "Rick will be going to Princeton, you know," Dad explained. Sizing up two suckers for an easy sale, the salesman took out a wool three-piece suit and threw in an orange dress shirt—"for Princeton, you know"—that would have appalled any dyed-in-the-wool preppy. And this was conservative Pasadena.

What did a Californian see when he showed up for Freshman Week? A bunch of kids acting prematurely old. Their madras shorts were faded and their loafers scuffed; at least mine were brand-new. They hung old hunting prints on their walls. Wouldn't a Beatles poster do? They dangled their father's or grandfather's class banners out their windows, claiming their place in Princeton's past, if not its Old-Fogeydom. They might have blasted Crosby Stills Nash & Young out those same leaded windows, but they were hosting each other at cocktail parties. Cocktail parties? Who ever heard of an eighteen-year-old throwing a cocktail party?

I'd spent the summer reading *Crime and Punishment*, thinking I could catch up with kids who'd floated through AP exams. There was one incredibly sophisticated girl in my freshman literature seminar at Princeton who wore horn-rimmed glasses and had blonde hair that fell over her eyes—she'd actually gone to school with Carol. She intimidated me with her references to things like "structuralism" and "deconstruction," more words I had to look up.

Fortunately I found my place on campus through singing: God's gift to me, a decent singing voice. Would that I would use it wisely and well. For many years that was my prayer, even at times when I didn't believe in God. That I wouldn't squander something that was beyond my own achieving, especially in a family where no one was particularly musical. No concert violinists or jazz pianists in the gene pool, not even a barbershop quartet singer.

At Princeton I discovered several groups that seemed glad to have an extra tenor. I sang in Freshman Singers, the Princeton Glee Club, the Chapel Choir, the student-written Triangle Show, and most important, one of the all-male a cappella groups. I was never a great sight-reader and could never get my line right until the third or fourth pass. "We'll call you Melody Hamlin," the guys in the a cappella group said. "All you're good for is the melody."

"Melody Hamlin" became one of my nicknames (along with "Hambone" shortened to "Bones" which morphed into "Bonus" or just "Ness" in the happy absurdity of nicknames).

Through the group I became friends with some of the same people whose preppy behavior had seemed such a mystery. I learned that a threadbare tweed jacket with elbow patches was much better than anything brand-new from a department store, and that long-sleeve, button-down shirts were best worn when un-ironed. Ties should be narrow, the narrower the better. I'd learned the code so well that when my parents came to visit my junior year, I looked with alarm at my father's wide tie and his huge lapels that could have been fins on a '57 Cadillac. What would my prepster friends think of me?

Had I become as much of a snob as that? I cringe at the memory.

Carol and I ended up in the same circle of friends, a wry, tight, witty bunch. She was part of the gang that went for a midnight dip—in our bathing suits—in the Woodrow Wilson School fountain spring of senior year, a certain rite of passage. We danced to Lester Lanin playing Cole Porter tunes at my eating club, Princeton's home-grown version of a Greek frat. (How quickly I had adopted the preppy ways.) She was there that May day before graduation when some of us drove down to Winterthur in Delaware—she might even have driven us in her old Saab. After touring the museum, with its American antiques, we stopped at a farm stand and bought baskets of fresh asparagus and strawberries. We cooked up the former for dinner—did we add some meat?—and had a party on a friend's dorm-room rooftop, listening to his recordings of Edith Piaf singing "La Vie en Rose" and "Je Ne Regrette Rien," the host crooning along and raising his eyebrows in a Gallic shrug.

Carol and I were friends, just good friends. She had a boyfriend at Yale, and I had recently broken up with a woman at Harvard, not because I wasn't madly in love with her but because I didn't see how we could really make it as a couple when I had no idea what I was going to do with my life, and, in my heart of hearts, I believed that the next woman I went out with would be the woman I married, closet traditionalist that I was.

My entire family came out from California to witness my graduation. There is a snapshot someone took of that day with both Carol and me beneath the elms in front of Nassau Hall, gazing in different directions in our caps and gowns. She looks worried, her brow furrowed, and I look distracted, searching for family members in the crowd. I packed my suitcases that afternoon, sent a trunk home, and then drove across the country with my parents in their new Volvo, not sure I'd ever see my East Coast friends again. I had to come up with a plan for some sort of future, and so that summer, while painting my sister's house, I decided to go to Italy and live there as long as the money held out.

Indeed I did, living in Florence for two years, supporting myself by teaching English as a foreign language and tutoring kids in the expatriate community. I studied voice with an opera singer and nurtured secret hopes of writing a Great American Novel, at least a slim one. All I ever wrote were a few self-absorbed entries in my journal and lots of letters home—cramming those cheap blue aerograms with my tiny script.

Some of those letters were addressed to Carol. She was working in book publishing in New York City, following a more conventional career path. Maybe I'd move to New York after Italy. We'd see each other there. Good friends. We were just good friends.

Carol is a brave woman. She has a lot of emotional courage, more than she will ever admit to. She was the one to make the first move, to actually spell it out, admitting that possibly, frankly we were more than friends, that maybe we were falling in love. Brave? Well, brave enough. She was a writer. She declared herself by mail.

By then I had been living in New York for over a year, pursuing a career as an actor/singer. In between dance classes and voice lessons and acting classes and auditions I caught up with that circle of Princeton friends of which she was a vital part. We saw each other at parties, put on a wedding shower for some friends, went to see movies, dropped in at museums.

For a while I was homeless, sleeping on friends' living room couches. When she took a ten-day trip she asked me to house-sit her 300-square-foot aerie at the top of an Upper West Side Art Deco tower. Want to fall in love with someone? Live for a while in their space. I studied the books in her bookshelf, gazed at the photos on her bureau, listened to her records, and was baffled by the makeup she'd left behind in the medicine cabinet. I could picture her at her typewriter, the wind whistling through the windows, the music of the recorder players from down-stairs wafting up through the floorboards. I cleaned her phone—she remembers this—scrubbing it of the grime that gets encrusted under the rotary dial, and bought her a colander so she could properly drain her pasta.

Later that year I found her a job as a desk clerk at an old residential hotel on Madison Avenue where I worked. She did the day shift, I did evenings. The place was clos-ing down. There were only thirty residents left. All we had to do was give them their mail and buzz them in the front door. It left plenty of time for her to polish up manu-scripts and me to memorize scenes for acting class.

She had left her full-time publishing job and was a freelance writer. Her first book was called *Fabulous Nails*, a guide for doing your fingernails. She had also created a page-a-day calendar of quotations. "I wouldn't have had the courage to do this without your support," she said in an unguarded moment.

"It's a no-brainer," I said. If anybody could make it as a writer, it was she. Not only was she talented, with a distinctive voice that was both funny and authoritative, but she was also incredibly self-disciplined, never one to miss a deadline. At Princeton she'd managed to finish her senior thesis six weeks early.

In the three years since college she had taken on a new style, trendier, more urban. Her once-blonde hair was now reddish, thanks to henna, and she had a great purple plastic raincoat, which I could admire when we changed shifts at the hotel.

One of the things I missed from college was running into people, catching up between classes. With Carol I had a regular rendezvous five days a week. I could find out what she was doing, what she was writing. She was contributing to a satiric take on preppydom called *The Official Preppy Handbook*. She ended up writing about a third of the book, for which she got an author's credit on the front page but no royalty or copyright, just a flat fee, a mistake she would never make again. It has long been out of print, but I can turn to passages in the sole copy on our shelves and hear her voice, her barbed wit in essays like "Prep Sex: A Contradiction in Terms" and even see her picture, in which she is dressed, improbably enough, as the "Amazon" ("Don't worry, I have problems with my backhand, too"). The book was a huge best seller, more often studied as a sartorial guide than satire. For Carol, it launched her career as a writer, humorist, social historian, and novelist.

My own acting career moved forward in fits and starts. I was lucky to get work doing church choir jobs, singing the occasional memorial service, appearing in an off-off-Broadway musical, doing summer stock. But even when I was taking on a dream role—Lieutenant Cable in *South Pacific*, Hero in *A Funny Thing Happened on the Way to the Forum*, Tony in *West Side Story*—I felt like I was only faking it. This was not my calling.

The brave courtship letter came when I was out in California, trying my luck on the West Coast. "It was probably a good thing that you left New York for a while," she wrote, "because I think I was falling in love with you..."

I stared at the typewritten page for a long time, dumbfounded. There was only one way to answer the letter, the truth: "I think I was falling in love with you too..." How did I know? How do you ever know? Maybe it was a fleeting moment when we were putting on that wedding shower for our mutual friends and we were in the kitchen of the old rambling West End Avenue apartment, where I slept in the maid's room, my only view an airshaft. I was her sous-chef, enamored of her culinary skills and what she could make of a three-by-five recipe card with her illegible fountain pen script on it. Or maybe it was when she gave me a copy of the page-a-day calendar she had created and discovered the quote she had put on my birthday, "A strong response to art is like money in a Swiss bank. You can never go emotionally bankrupt," a line I'd treasured by Kenneth Clark.

It might have been when we went shopping on one of the coldest days of the year for the cheapest upright piano I could find, and as I watched her breath take form in the brilliant blue of a frigid New York sky, a blue that matched her eyes, I was seeing beauty I had mistakenly taken for granted. It went back to house-sitting in her apartment and wanting to know more about the books stacked next to her bed. She gave me the sense that somehow I counted with her, that I had made a difference, that she wouldn't have taken this risk and called herself a writer if I hadn't believed in her. I did believe in her, sometimes more than I believed in myself. Was this something we were meant to do together?

"Creator, Redeemer and Lover." To know God's love through the abiding affection of an earthly lover. To know that God's love is that big and that immediate and that personal. God my Lover was moving in my life, making me change, turning me around, bringing me closer to the person I was called to be.

I lingered in California, getting a job as a spear-carrier in a production of *The Merchant of Venice* and then signing on to do children's theater, a couple of performances a day. I made enough to pay for the gas in the hand-me-down Toyota I drove. All the while, Carol and I kept up a torrid correspondence, letting our words do the difficult work of taking us from the comfort zone of good friends to the danger zone of lovers. Feeling freer because of distance, we shared everything on the page. We were hesitant about talking on the phone—would the sound of our voices separate us?—but kept up the writing.

Neither she nor I has ever dared reread all the letters

we wrote back then. At the time we said that someday we'd collect and print them in a romantic volume for lovers only, a lavender-colored collection of purple prose. Falling in love can be thrilling and terrifying at once. And the most terrifying thought of all: What if it hadn't turned out all right? What if we hadn't forged this unbreakable bond? What if Carol hadn't sent that first letter? What if I hadn't responded?

And what now if I left her, making a premature exit from a hospital bed?

Faith mattered to both of us. That came through on the page. She didn't share my Presbyterian heritage— she'd grown up Episcopalian, and nothing was going to change that—but we were both inveterate churchgoers. We believed in worship, at the very least, as Kurt Vonnegut Jr. famously put it, for the chance to "daydream about God." Religion was a tool to help us find our place in the cosmos. In one letter she described seeing a documentary about an order of nuns that had left her weeping and wondering how she could find some holy calling. She took up a volunteering assignment through her church, visiting an old Irish woman in a walk-up in the East Eighties, Henrietta, who taught her how to knit.

After four months of writing back and forth we knew we had to see each other. I had spring break off from the children's theater gig and booked a flight to New York to see Carol and see if what we had was really all it had become on the page. I took the red-eye and arrived on

Palm Sunday morning, when Central Park is just turning the light green that is called "spring green" in a box of crayons, the forsythia the bravest bit of color. We sat on a bench in the wan sun and watched the daffodils tremble in the breeze.

We had that week together, that perfect week when we dodged running into anyone we knew—at one point actually hiding behind a newsstand—for fear that what we had discovered between us wasn't quite ready for public consumption. We wanted to save it for ourselves.

Not for nothing did Jesus urge us to go into our closets and pray. "Go into your room and shut the door and pray to your Father who is in secret; and your Father who sees in secret will reward you." Sometimes our deepest yearnings are too fragile to share with anyone else but God.

There would be a long back-and-forth courtship, with a trying long-distance relationship until I moved back to New York for good and gave up all designs on an acting career. I joined the choir at the Episcopal church where she sang—where we still sing—and we got married there on the last day of April, but I still think of Palm Sunday as our anniversary.

CHAPTER FIVE

Hospital, Day 4

In between sleep and groggy wakefulness, in between a million doctor visits and nurses coming and going, I looked across the room, and Carol was still there, as constant as the IV drip in my arm and the blood pressure cuff that lurched into life at some unexplained signal, expanding and contracting on my bicep. *I'm sorry to be doing this to you. I'm sorry you have to be here. I'm sorry you have to worry and wonder and pray and send out all those e-mail messages and I'm grateful for them, sweetie.* "Sweetie," our word for each other, the one we use when no one is listening.

Don't apologize, her eyes tell me. *Don't go there. This is what I do. This is what I promised to do. This is what you would do.*

"For better for worse, for richer or poorer, in sickness and in health, to love and to cherish, till death us do part," we promised back then, when we couldn't possibly know what all that would entail. We were young, in our midtwenties. We knew enough about poorer. I became a freelance writer that first year of marriage and earned all of three thousand dollars. As for sickness, well, I was healthy. I still think of myself that way. On any questionnaire I've had to fill out where it says "health" I still check the box that says "excellent." Is that idle fantasy or faith at work? I remember being chided by my dermatologist for not checking the box that said "skin cancer."

"But that was just basal cell stuff you took off," I said. "Everybody has that. Anybody who grew up in the sun in California."

"It's carcinoma," he said, truth-teller that he is. "That's cancer. That's why I took it off."

Now I was not healthy, and Carol had to do this with me. In the hospital I was praying through her. She was my contact with the outer world and my contact with this inner world of doctors and nurses and aides and therapists. She had to ask the questions that I would never have thought to ask even if I could talk. She would understand the answers and their significance.

So much of marriage is this in-the-trenches work. Did you pay the Con Ed bill? What did Verizon say about our wonky signal? Are we free to go over to dinner at Scott and Katie's on Saturday? How is your mom? We're about to run out of toilet paper...OK, I'll put it on the marketing list. In a hospital the nuts-and-bolts of it is cranked up.

Note to self: may my loved ones always know they are loved.

Would you do it again, sweetie, if you knew how many times you would have to play the caregiver? In sickness and in health, indeed. When Frank Sinatra got married the last time, to his richest wife, he was said to have repeated the line "for richer" with glee. Would anyone say the same about "in sickness"?

She is horrified at the prospect that I will predecease her. Just on the basis of demographics, that's likely. Women outlive men. You see it every time you visit an old folks' home. "It just doesn't seem fair," she says. "Why would God bring two people together only to tear them apart?"

"Life is a gift," I want to say. "Right to life" is a phrase of faulty theological logic. Life is a gift, not a divine right.

If there's a spiritual lesson in sickness it must be that you can't make yourself well. You're out of control. You did all those things you were supposed to do to be healthy. You ate right (mostly), you got plenty of exercise (generally), you tried to get enough sleep, but what does all that matter when you're on your back in a hospital bed? You can't *do* anymore. You have to *be*. You have to let go and trust God and trust your doctors. You're at their mercy.

Day four, the routine had settled in. I would wake up after a bad night of sleep. Carol would walk down from our apartment. I would pretend to eat the food on my breakfast tray—the cereal, a roll with butter, juice, lukewarm tea—and we would greet whoever showed up. We might have been actors in a drama for them, the man in the bed with a mystery illness, the wife who wasn't sleeping or eating enough. But they were actors in a drama for us, too.

The day nurse arrived and scrawled his/her name on the whiteboard, erasing the name of the night nurse. Then they would take my vitals, recording them in some computer.

"What are you going…to do…tomorrow?" I asked Jay. He lived in New Jersey. Like most of the nurses, he worked twelve-hour shifts three or four days a week.

"Work around the house and ride my motorcycle."

"With...a helmet?"

"Never. I'm hoping to be a patient someday. So I can get treated like you."

We needed our jokes.

"When I come back, I'm giving you a shower."

"Can't...wait."

Dr. Chang, the attending, came at the beginning of the day and returned again at the end. She reminded me of a piano teacher, the sort who would listen to you play an entire piece all the way through, without interrupting, and then make a few salient points about your fingering or phrasing.

She could explain why a certain test was ordered and why some medicine was being administered or why a different specialist had appeared. I trusted her. I wanted stars and smiley faces on her report.

There was the newly minted resident who must have worked under her in internal medicine. Not much older than our twenty-eight-year-old son Will, he had a hipster beard and an easy bedside manner. A graduate of Middlebury, he'd grown up in Colorado and had doctors in his genes. I felt that I was collaborating on his education and advancement as a doctor, fully invested in his success.

I wanted to please all my doctors, to be at my best when they appeared no matter how rotten I felt, to be such a good patient that they would willingly come back as often as possible. The patient/doctor relationship is oddly symbiotic. Even with the younger doctors, like this one,

I was glad to let them be the authority, the oracle, if they pleased. "I will get better for you," I would think, "thanks to all the prayers, and then I hope you can take credit for it." I would be the perfect pupil, wanting their achievements to reflect well on the teacher.

Some doctors *were* teachers. An older specialist would come by my bedside with a few medical students in tow. These visits confused the doctor/patient dynamic. Who was the student now? The specialist would look at me but at the same time he/she was performing for the fresh young minds who were taking in my situation. In the worst of these situations, the specialist would speak to his charges as though I weren't even there. I felt like a piece of meat. Chopped liver.

It was good that Carol had requested no visitors because these doctor visits were taxing enough. In each case I hoped to rise to the occasion. Patients can have performance anxiety too.

Seth the internist came by—dear Seth—more than once. I don't know how he found the time. I still had his Columbia-Presbyterian sweatshirt. I told him I'd give it back if he ever wanted it, although I couldn't imagine he'd take it with the new exotic germs I'd left on it.

The team of pulmonologists was confusing. There were a couple of residents who appeared, and an authoritative older doctor, but never the woman, Dr. DiMango, who was the specialist I went to. I liked her a lot. In fact, I credited her with saving my life eight years earlier. She'd ordered a CT scan for a persistent cough. When she got the results she called my home first—warning enough—and then got me at the office. "Your lungs are fine," she said in her no-nonsense way, "but you'd better do something about that aneurysm in your aorta." Aneurysm in my aorta? Talk about scary. Open-heart surgery came ten days later.

"We've talked to Dr. DiMango," the pulmonologists would say. "We've shared your test results with her." Keeping her in the loop.

I liked the infectious disease guy, although he was pretty dorky. Dorky can be reassuring in a hospital setting. Carol claimed that his lab coat wasn't very clean. There was an intern who visited almost every day, lingering in the room as though we were his parents, which we could easily have been. "Parents can die," I thought. "Parents can get sick and fall apart and land in hospitals where all the king's horses and all the king's men can't put them back together again. Beware."

The rheumatologists...well, I've mentioned them. There was the crepe hanger, a little stooped, pursing her lips and shaking her head, but the younger one was very thoughtful, engaging, hopeful. She reminded me of a really smart travel agent who can book a trip, recommend just the right hotel, and tell you about a garden or museum you should visit. As if I were going anywhere.

My beloved Italian cardiologist, Dr. Ravalli, appeared. He's Roman from Rome, *romano da Roma*, and he kindly tolerates my attempts at Italian. The first time I met him

66

we talked about Italy for twenty minutes in the exam room before he delivered the bad news that I would indeed have to have open-heart surgery. That aneurysm needed to be fixed soon, right away, in fact. I've come to see that this chattiness is his healing touch, to take me away from my fears and remind me of the Piazza Navona, the Castel Sant'Angelo, the Pantheon, a plate of fresh pasta. He's also a runner, lean like a runner, and I consult him on things like plantar fasciitis and sore knees (he's tried acupuncture). I like to hear about what his kids are doing and how they've grown up, Italians in New York. We sometimes run into him at the supermarket down by the Hudson River on Sunday, shopping with his tan, coiffed, unmistakably Roman wife.

He looked concerned now.

That fourth day, Wednesday, Carol and Tim counted how many people checked on me between 9:00 in the morning and 5:00 in the evening. Fifty-four people, fifty-four people who wanted to help me as much as I wanted to be helped. I didn't tell any of them the secret holy plot that I was going to get better and get out of here. They were just supposed to keep me alive.

I couldn't always quite believe the message myself. That seems to be a spiritual quandary. You accept something as a divine truth, it has stirred in your soul, whether at a dark moment or light, and then, days later, although you still believe it, you wonder how it could possibly happen; faith surging, faith waning.

The underground pipeline was working. My spirit was being ministered to by more prayers than I could fathom. But part of me didn't want to fathom them. It would be too scary to have to take in all that love, to have to receive it. I preferred being the giver, not the receiver. A closeted control freak, I'd rather ask you how *you* are doing than have to tell you how *I* am. I find it hard to trust that others are all that interested in what I might say about myself. It's a wonder that I can receive God's love at all.

Sometime in the middle of that day, that Wednesday, some brief moment when it was just Carol and me, I brought up the trip we were supposed to make to California the next week. There was a big conference planned. We were both supposed to speak, and Carol would be one of the keynote speakers.

"You should...go...to California without me," I said.

She looked at me like I was crazy.

"I'll be OK here...There are people looking after me..."

"I'm not going to go," she said.

"You should... They need you... They're counting on you."

I felt guilty about being sick. It was a work thing, an obligation. At least I was clear-eyed enough to realize I wasn't going to make it. But Carol could go in my place.

"I have to stay here," she said, telling me that I was much more important than work, that love came first. I could hardly take it in. It would have been enough to say "Thank you," but I didn't. Not then.

You see what I mean about receiving.

When Timothy was four years old and in that hospital bed for twenty-six days, his leg in traction, I had my own medical problem that was wending its way through diagnosis. A tumor in my parotid gland, probably benign, as the doctor said, holding up one finger warningly to calm my nerves, but it would have to come out.

"This is not a very good time," I told him. "Our four-year-old son is in the hospital right now, twenty-six days in traction. He broke his femur."

"We need to do this surgery," he said. "You shouldn't wait."

"But my wife and I are scrambling. Our other son, the older one, has chicken pox and is at home recovering from that. Between the two of them and the two of us we're with one of them each night. We don't want to leave them alone."

"It'll be an out-patient procedure," he said, ever calmingly. "We can do it during the day, and you'll be free to be with him at night. What hospital is he at?"

"The Hospital for Joint Diseases on Seventeenth Street."

"We can do your surgery just a couple of blocks away."

Just as I'd feared, disasters coming in threes, an unholy trinity. We had our third now, in case we were looking for one. The surgeon, as surgeons do, I've come to see, played down the need for any recovery time and played up the routine nature of the operation. They'd take out the tumor in an afternoon, and that would be that. All the better that we had all these medical problems going on at once. We could take care of them all at once.

So in the middle of Tim's hospital sojourn I had surgery. The tumor came out, but I had no idea how awful you could feel coming out of anesthesia. Carol couldn't be there with me because she was with Tim—the babysitter was with Will at home. The operation went longer than expected, and the surgery was complicated. I woke up in the recovery room well after 6:00 p.m. to find a friend from church at my bedside. No telling how long she had been there.

"Rick," she said. "Rick, it's Auntie Margaret."

She had been a nurse with years of experience behind her at one of the top New York hospitals. Besides that, she was a diligent praying person, a pillar of the church, the woman at coffee hour who always made sure there were enough cookies and cheese and crackers and coffee stirrers to keep the postworship crowd happy.

"*Ugggggggh*," I groaned. I had bandages wrapped around my face, like some wounded soldier in a Civil War drama.

"I have to go," she said.

"How long have you been here?" I tried to ask.

"The surgery went well. You're going to be fine. But you'll need to spend the night here to recover."

I nodded. What would Carol do? How would we manage?

"I've called Carol. She's got someone to stay with William."

We were loved—we *are* loved. Friends from church, friends from work, old friends from college, pitched in and helped out. Mom had already gone home, having done her stint. This time Dad came out, flying out on the red-eye, stepping out of the yellow cab in his red sweater vest.

All the nerves in my face were bruised. My smile was lopsided, my face sagged. I needed to use my hand to help close one eye. "The nerves will come back," the doctor promised. "None have been damaged. They're just stunned."

He described enough of the operation that I had to admire how he'd done it, removing the tumor through the threadlike nerves without damaging any of them.

"But was the tumor cancerous?" I asked.

"It didn't look like it, but we'll find out." He held up his calming index finger, waving it up to heaven. "Don't worry."

Carol and I didn't see each other for a week. One of us would be at home, one of us would be at the hospital with Tim, and we traveled back and forth on the subway when our babysitter Sharon could spell us at home. The first time Carol saw me was at the hospital, and she was so horrified by the sight of my nerve-stunned face that she went out and bought a black dress, sure of her impending widowhood. In sickness or in health, indeed.

I remember sleeping in Timothy's hospital room at night, looking out at New York's never-dark sky from my cot by the window and thinking—praying—"You know, if

I die, I will be glad that this is one of the last things I do. To be by my son at his bedside."

The tumor, I was finally told, was benign.

September 16, 5:16 p.m.

Well, we all knew Rick was special, right? How special? SO special that the best medical minds at Columbia-Presbyterian Hospital still can't figure out what the heck he has. At least there was no talk of birds today. The three areas of focus are 1/reaction to antibiotics given for a boil last week (inglorious, that boil). 2/strange infection (really, really strange) or 3/autoimmune disorder. Many of the tests for the last take a long time to "cook." That's what they say, "cook."

More and more objects cluttering up this space. Oxygen machine, IV pole, device to squeeze his calf muscles since he can't get up, commode (why is it here if he can't get up?), spare tank of oxygen...not to mention the usual bed, table, and monitors.

And so busy! Tim and I have been keeping a tally of the individuals who cross the threshold to minister to Rick. Between 9:00 a.m. and 5:00 p.m. it's 54.

And I have to say, they've all been great.

He's still really sick. Didn't have a fever until late this afternoon, so that's good. On lots of drugs, lots of fluid, and most importantly, lots of oxygen.

Keep the prayers and good thoughts coming, dear friends.

CHAPTER SIX

Day 4, Evening

That night I had a roommate in the hospital, an older guy—maybe not that much older than me but old enough to seem older. He was on the other side of the curtain they pulled around my bed, but I could hear him wheezing. He'd had to wait in the ER for a long time before being admitted. On oxygen like me, he sounded like he was wearing a mask, not just tubes stuck in his nose. The oxygen machine hissed.

I wanted to talk to him through the curtain.

"Have you been here before?"

"Yeah, this happens to me a lot. I'm on oxygen at home. Carry around a tank with me, but sometimes that's not enough. I start wheezing and carrying on. I have to call for an ambulance, and they bring me here."

"Does it scare you?"

"Sure. But they've always been able to help me here. I get better and then I go home. That's what will happen this time."

I could see myself in some vague future, like this guy, carrying around a tank of oxygen everywhere I went, to the office, on the subway, a special pass allowing me to take it on the airplane. The bother of it, the comfort of it, the wonder of modern medicine, the pain of it, prolonging life, postponing death, the spirit struggling to catch up with the body. Compassion flooded me.

"Are you going to be OK?"

"Of course. It just takes time. I like this hospital."

"So do I. My kids were born here."

"You've got kids?"

"Two of them. Boys, twenty-eight and twenty-five. The twenty-eight-year-old is coming tomorrow to see me. He lives in San Francisco."

"Nice."

"He was the answer to prayer. Like all kids." I couldn't ever forget my blessings. Especially now. Count them at night like counting sheep when you can't sleep.

Those fifteen blocks from the hospital to our apartment had seemed like sacred ground back then. In the pre-dawn of a mild March morning I made that trip, barely able to contain myself. "My son is born," I would announce to the homeless guy in a refrigerator box near the Armory. "We just had a baby," I would tell the sanitation workers throwing trash into the garbage truck. The lady delivering a stack of morning papers was surely just waiting to hear: "It's a boy!"

It was too early to find a cab or catch a bus, and besides, I had to walk off the adrenaline. A miracle had happened. I'd just held our baby wrapped like a burrito in his blanket, pink-faced, wrinkly, tiny, brand-new and old-looking all at once. I had to sleep, but who could sleep now? How could you sleep when you were so full of hope? I was scared out of my wits and not at all sure I was up to the task the good Lord had given me, and yet certain that this was the best role I was ever meant to take on. Dad.

Courage is fear that has said its prayers, as the saying goes, and the prayers were being uttered with each footstep.

"There were two of us in that birthing room, and then there were three, and he's always going to be there. Forever, or as long as we live. He looks like he's smart, the way he turned his head, and he's got a pair of lungs, the way he cried. Do you think he'll be a singer? Or with those tiny arms, a slugger? Will I know enough to teach him how to play ball?"

William Sloane Coffin, senior minister at Riverside Church when I sang in the choir there, used to announce at every baptism that a newborn was God's way of telling the world that it was meant to go on. Then Coffin would look at the flushed faces of the proud parents, the two wreathed in smiles, and remark how these people were taking on the biggest responsibilities of their lives. Look how happy they were. Thrilled, ecstatic. "That's because," he would go on, "it's not our freedoms that give us the greatest pleasure. It's our responsibilities."

Lesson learned. All these responsibilities would make me happy. I can't imagine what life would have been like if we hadn't had children. But it was never a sure thing.

Carol and I gave our baby a name before he was born,

before we knew we could even have a child. Truax, we called him. Truax, after some family name we found on an old genealogical chart. Truax, because we knew we'd never ever call a child by that name.

We refused to contemplate having a child until we had a place big enough to house a child, unlike the one-bedroom, third-floor walk-up we first called home. "This apartment isn't big enough to change your mind in," someone once said. So we began looking and came uptown to Washington Heights at the suggestion of a friend, wondering if we could raise a Truax here.

When we checked out apartments, I would go into the extra bedroom, the one that would be "the office" until it became "the nursery," and I'd make a lot of noise. I'd pretend to be Truax, jumping up and down, singing songs from some dreamed-up crib. "How noisy is it from the other bedroom?" I asked. "Can you hear Truax in there?"

We did it ostensibly to test the acoustics of our potential home, no doubt to the annoyance of the real-estate broker, but we were also testing ourselves, looking to the time when we would have children, when we would be parents awakened in the middle of the night by a real-life Truax crying at the end of the hall. Who would he or she be? Who would *we* be?

We remembered something, some good advice we'd received from the minister who'd married us. No, it wasn't Dr. Coffin, but the old bachelor rector of the Episcopal church where we worshipped and still worship today. Our premarital counseling was shortened into one cover-all-the-basics session over a glass of sherry in the living room of his down-at-the-heels rectory.

He circled back to the topic of children. What did he know about them? After all, he was a single man in his sixties, never married. We put down our sherry glasses and listened politely. "If you have children—and they are a blessing," he said as though to remind himself that it was true, "make sure you're happy. If you are happy, your children will be happy."

The message was clear: Be ready to sacrifice everything for your children, but don't sacrifice your marriage. The happiness you have as a couple, your love for each other, your care and concern for each other, will be the happiness your children experience growing up. You could give them everything, every material advantage, but if you don't give them that, the home they have will not be happy.

We chose a two-bedroom apartment in an aging complex fifteen blocks north of the hospital. It was of mock-Tudor design, reddish brick and half-timbering covered by ivy, with an overgrown garden of roses and hydrangeas and a small playground for kids. By the time we moved in Carol was pregnant—*we* were pregnant—and she needed to be careful. Our one mover and I carried most of our boxes of books, our greatest treasures, up the flight of stairs. We looked out the casement windows to a sliver of the Hudson, framed between two taller apartment buildings.

Two out-of-work actors painted the kitchen and living room. One of them, the less prepossessing of the pair, went on to become famous, appearing in dozens of movies, and for years afterward we regretted throwing out the sun-dried tomatoes he had left in our fridge. We could have said, "Those are Stanley Tucci's sun-dried tomatoes."

Everything we saw now was colored by our expecting, our waiting, our hoping, our dreaming, our praying. Dreaming is praying—hard to do in a hospital bed when your oxygen numbers are sliding and your fever is rising. But back then, could I remember how it was, how I saw the world?

Would our baby—would Truax—slide on the slide in that playground or climb the jungle gym? Would I push him on that swing? Would the baby in that stroller become one of his friends someday? The neighborhood was full of older German-Jewish residents who had moved here before and after World War II, finding sanctuary in the New World. They lined the park benches, reading the *Frankfurter Zeitung* or the Yiddish *Forward*, and I readily cast a half dozen of them as surrogate grandparents.

We were happy without children and told ourselves that if we didn't get pregnant we would still be happy, and that if we did, it was meant to be, God's idea as much as ours. But as the days ticked by, the prospect became scarier and scarier. Everybody asked Carol how she was feeling. Did she have morning sickness? Did she get tired? Could she feel the baby moving inside? Nobody asked what I was going through. If they had, I would have exploded.

"I'm scared to death," I would have said. "How are we ever going to afford a new baby? How are we going to feed it, clothe it, send it to nursery school and kindergarten? How will we pay for piano lessons and ballet classes and gymnastic classes, let alone college?" I didn't mind economizing for myself. I could take homemade salami sandwiches to the office for the rest of my life and buy my jackets and sweaters at the church rummage sale, but I couldn't do that for Truax. He'd need new shoes and a Happy Meal.

One Saturday I went to Woolworth's and bought a plastic trash basket for Truax's room. THE VERY CHEAPEST ONE I COULD FIND. I saved a dollar and ninety-nine cents. I brought it back and put it in his room and realized how ridiculous I was being. The money wasn't the issue. It was the fear of not measuring up, not being patient enough or loving or caring enough to be a parent. A friend visited with his toddler, and the kid pulled every book within reach off the bookshelves. I watched the man calmly put all the books back. "I'll never be able to do that," I thought.

We bought the baby furniture: a crib, a chest of drawers, a toy chest, and a changing table. The latter was the most intimidating, with its drawers for diapers, baby powder, and wipes. It was hard to believe I'd ever know how to use them. But the dreaming part of expecting caught up with us when Carol painted the chest of drawers and toy chest with white enamel, stenciling letters in primary colors across it: "A, B, C, D, E, F, G, H..." I could imagine the day when I would point to them and ask Truax, "What letter is that?" and he would say, "Daddy, that's *A...B... C.*" I would take him to Disney movies. I would show Truax how to ride a bicycle in the little park. He would play in the sandbox. He would squeal with delight when I caught him at the bottom of the slide.

I would be called Daddy or Dad or Pop or the old man. Suddenly I would belong to someone else, the way I belonged to Carol. She joked about how she would be able to refer to me in the third person, talking to Truax, about "your father." As in "Your father will change your diapers this time" or "Your father will take you to the park this morning." This new triangulation: my husband, my son...your father. In families we claim each other and remind each other of how we're connected, just like Jesus saying to the disciples, "The Father and I are one."

The weather turned warm. Truax was late. It was early March, and suddenly there was a premature burst of spring. The kids in the neighborhood played their boom boxes in the park, the Latino strains of salsa echoed against the buildings near the hospital. The oldsters took their aluminum chairs outside, set up tables, and played dominoes. The medical students jogged in shorts up the hill. The weather wouldn't hold, we all knew that, but while it was spring it should be enjoyed. At dawn on the seventh of March, with sunshine streaming in the windows, Carol got up early and lingered in bed, propped up against the pillows.

"Is this it?" I asked.

"I think so," she said.

Is this it? Like me asking the same question years later, sick in bed, wondering if I was dying, wondering if now was the time to rush to the hospital.

Truax was ten days overdue. Were we ready? Of course not, but we were tired of waiting.

I tried to remember all that we'd learned from the birthing classes. I was supposed to be Carol's coach, timing the contractions and helping her through the pain with breathing and relaxation techniques. For a moment I envied the dads of our parents' generation who didn't have to enter birthing rooms but paced hospital halls instead, cigars in their pocket.

"Can I get you anything?" I asked, hoping to sound solicitous.

"Maybe some videos to watch." We could hang out at home and make sure these contractions were the real ones. One hated to sound a false alarm. You didn't want to look like a fool, like going to the ER with a chest infection and being told it was nothing. On the other hand, maybe this was just the moment to look like a fool—part of the cosmic preparation of parenthood, part of life.

"What about some exercise?" I asked.

The teacher of the birthing classes, a big cheerful Irish woman with ruddy cheeks and a nurse's frankness about body parts, had said it was good to walk during those early stages of labor. Exercise could move things along.

"It's only seven in the morning," Carol said.

"It's supposed to be good for you," I said, taking on my coach role.

"OK."

I put on my jeans and a jacket, Carol wore her down overcoat, but to my mind's eye we looked like a pair auditioning for a Christmas pageant: Woman about to give birth to child, helpless husband standing by. All we lacked was a donkey and a manger. Every now and then we'd stop on the sidewalk and check our watches. Were the contractions coming quicker? Was today going to be the day?

The crocuses in the park were blooming, the azaleas were budding with pink crepe paper colors. I wondered if we would bring our kid—our Truax—here in another week or two. Would we be the proud couple pushing our newborn along the graveled walk?

A neighbor jogged past and stopped. "Carol," she asked, "are you in labor?"

How did she know? "Yes," Carol said.

Squeals of delight. "I won't tell anyone, I promise," our friend said. She'd been through it all herself, had a two-year-old daughter down the street. We walked back to the apartment, feeling like all eyes were on us. Our cover was blown. Would everybody in the neighborhood be looking out their windows to see when we would head off to the hospital? Were they timing our contractions too? Carol likes to believe that she is inconspicuous in any crowd. All at once she felt stared at. So did I, Mr. Soon-to-be-Dad.

That's part of it. You're having a baby. Branded before anyone can even see your offspring. You're entering a great unselective club that will give you instant rapport with more than half the world. Your heart will go out to the parent with the wailing child on the airplane because you know what it's like. You will feel nothing but pity for the mom or dad comforting the kid with spilled ice cream at the amusement park. No baby sounds exactly like another, but every parent's anguish is something you know.

Labor lasted all day, with videos and walks around the apartment, ice chips and phone calls to the doctor's office. By early evening we figured it was time to go. I picked up the bag that had been packed for weeks, and we called a cab to take us to the ER—quicker at finding it back then than twenty-eight years later.

We were taken up to the labor rooms in Babies Hospital. The efficient nurse checked Carol out. Only two centimeters dilated. "It'll be a while," she said, looking at us as though we were amateurs, which, let's face it, we were. Parents are all amateurs. "You live in the neighborhood," she observed. "You're better off waiting at home." It was like studying for an exam for weeks and being told you've flunked on the first question. Sent home.

We watched more videos and clocked the time between

contractions, Carol's misery increasing, but every time I suggested we go back to the hospital she rejected the idea. No more humiliation. She wasn't going to be sent home twice. We watched a 1950s movie that I couldn't begin to follow. "Now?" I kept asking Carol. No, not yet, not now. It was well after 10:00 p.m. when we headed back to the hospital, and we had to take the bus—couldn't even find a cab. The bus ride, my moment of humiliation.

"At least I'll be able to get something at the hospital for the pain," Carol said between contractions. She has always welcomed every official opportunity for pain relief.

"I'm afraid you're too far along," said the nurse when we arrived. "It's too late to do an epidural."

There were shouts in Spanish from the woman in the birthing room next door. Carol and I looked at each other with concern. Soon the shouts were coming from Carol. I couldn't for a moment remember what we were supposed to do with the breathing exercises. Wasn't she supposed to blow out and count when it came time for the pushing? Some coach I was.

The obstetrician on call waltzed in from a Saturday night dinner party, took off his jacket, and loosened his bow tie. With a few more pushes, suddenly the baby was born. Our boy. Our baby. Born early on a Sunday morning, Sunday's child. What we had waited for and wished for and prayed for was now more real than we could imagine. He cried right away, his face red from the unpleasantness of having to come out from that place where he had everything taken care of to this world where he'd have to work to get it. That happy, lusty, painful, joyful, miserable shout. He was here. Not Truax. The fake name disappeared in an instant. This baby was for real.

Carol took him in her arms. "He's beautiful," she said, and he was, in his blotchy, scrawny way. All these years later when I look at him, I can still see in his grown face that baby he was in the birthing room. Better than any dreams we ever had for him, how incomplete our hopes had been.

The nurse wrapped him up in a blanket, whisked him away, and then brought him back so we could admire him, and we still do. Finally I kissed Carol good-bye and walked back through the darkened neighborhood, buoyed by hopes, by love, by the magnitude of what had happened. I was full of thankfulness at every block, wreathed in smiles like the parents at baptisms who are told that every child is God's way of telling the world that it should go on. I would call his grandparents, waking them up as they would want to be awakened, letting them know they had a new grandchild, this one named after both his grandfathers, William and Thornton. William Thornton Hamlin.

CHAPTER SEVEN

Hospital, Day 5

September 17, 4:51 p.m.

Will arrived from SF this morning with his hipster haircut and his math-oriented brain, and he was the one who got the rheumatologists' report, which he saw as a "mapping" approach to problem-solving. Basically, the infectious-disease guys tested tons of viral and bacterial infections and came up with nothing, so autoimmune disorders seem more likely. As we know, their tests take longer. (And by the way, they don't really cook the results, so disappointing. That Was a Metaphor.) They expect information in the next couple of days, some of which won't be as clear-cut as the yes/no info from infections. So if your mind works like Will's, maybe you see this graphically.

Short version: still no diagnosis.

So, yes, this is like living in an episode of "House," but a really boring one with uniformly nice characters and no drug addiction and nobody having sex in the supply closet, which I know because it's right outside our door.

However—Rick walked today.

That, my friends, is epic. Walked twice around the nurses' station. And twice today docs have nudged down the oxygen flow in his machine, and his absorption has remained steady. He is also eating like a starving man. Best of all, we aren't very interesting anymore. Docs come in, look at his color, look at his numbers, ask how he feels, and with a cheerful smile, leave for a sicker patient. Being boring has never felt so good.

So you see, all those prayers and good wishes? They seem to be working. Not that you should stop: there's still a long way to go. Stay tuned!

Lots of love to all of you from the step-down unit.—Carol

Normally if our grown boys are coming home we want to put the best face on it, at least for that first night's homecoming. I wash their bedroom windows, I vacuum, I clean out a shelf in the medicine cabinet, I scrub the sink and wipe down the tile in the shower. We want to look our best for our kids. We roast the fatted calf, we buy a box of their favorite cereal. Will, for one, always asks me about my work. I tell him, putting the best spin on things.

But there is no spin you can put on for a hospital visit. You can't shield your child from a scary fact: you are going to check out someday and, chances are, it'll be through a series of medical setbacks, demanding a series of hospital visits. "No, don't come," you might want to say, but you yearn to see them, to hear from them, to have one more conversation with them.

"Hey, Will," I said wanly. Did I ever truly believe that courage is fear that has said its prayers?

"Hi, Dad," he said, giving me a hug through the spaghetti of wires coming out of my chest and the tubes attached to my nose, giving me air.

Most of all I wanted to shield him from the fear. "This is the hospital where you were born, Will," I wanted to say. "Think of what a joyful place it was for us then. It can still be that way. Not the way it is or feels now. This is only temporary, a little setback. I'm going to get better. It's ordained. You'll see."

Tim's way of dealing with the fear was to pray from the Book of Psalms in one corner. For Will it was using his quantitative skills, cataloging what the doctors were saying, creating in his head some Excel spreadsheet. Carol and I and Tim still wanted to see this as a narrative with an unwieldy cast of characters and a fuzzy plotline; Will would make sense of it the way he made sense of challenges at work, gathering information, categorizing it, asking questions, creating lists.

The first doctor of the day came in, started asking me some questions, then looked over at William and asked, "Is it OK to talk about this in front of him?"

"Of course," I said. "This is William, my oldest son."

William took down what the doctor said, his fingers flying across his computer. He would share with Carol everything. No secrets needed to be hid from my children.

My sons, my sons, you are my legacy. No book I ever

write, no speech I ever give, no meeting I lead, no class I teach, will ever mean as much to me. You are what I leave behind, and I pour my love into you. At my sixtieth birthday party, only months before, both William and Timothy had roasted me royally in witty toasts. But then Tim said, "I'm not sure what I'm going to do with my life but the one thing I know I want to be is a dad, and that's a mark of how good a dad my dad was." What more could you want? Might as well kiss it good-bye and leave it there. Go out on a high note.

Not here, not in this hospital bed.

"How was your flight?" I asked Will.

"Good, Dad."

"You sleep...on the red-eye?"

"I got in a couple of hours."

"Easier than...in a hospital."

William can't really hide it from us. Tough and cerebral in a business setting, he is a softie at the core, much more likely than Tim to burst into tears.

He picks his moments, and they bust you up. He did it the day of my dad's funeral.

Dad had died after a long, slow decline. "He gave us the luxury of saying good-bye," was how Mom put it.

The service was at a packed church, the place they had worshipped for years. All four of us kids spoke. We could look down from the chancel, where we were seated, to the front pew, where he had always sat, bellowing the hymns at top volume in his out-of-tune voice. "He had a few good notes," I said, "and sometimes they were the right notes." Mom beamed at us from the same pew. We all wore his trademark bow ties, raiding his closet, everyone taking their favorite ones. He had served in the submarine corps in World War II, and a few of the surviving crew members showed up with a wreath. I sang that day for him, choosing Rodgers & Hammerstein's "No Other Love" because the tune was used in the TV documentary *Victory at Sea*, and to Dad, any good piece of music sounded "just like *Victory at Sea*." This time it *was Victory at Sea*.

After the service we hosted a reception for 350 people and, at day's end, we returned to Mom and Dad's house, the modern one they had built after we kids flew the coop. That evening, at what was now Mom's house, William burst into tears. I was downstairs getting ready for bed, but I could hear him in the kitchen, a twenty-something crying like a kid who has struck out at bat. The grandfather he loved was gone and nothing would be the same again. "Oh, Will," I heard Carol say, "it's all right, honey."

I didn't want him to cry now at the hospital. Didn't want him to cry ever. How lousy of me to rattle his world. Parents die, parents get sick, security gets shaken. Every time I attempt to reconcile myself to the concept of death and its inevitability—how necessary it is, how essential—I circle back to this: what a terrible thing to do to the ones you leave behind.

I wanted to be strong for Will. Somehow being the Rock of Gibraltar mattered more to me with him than it did with Tim—maybe because William was the oldest and I felt more responsibility. He was my firstborn, the first one I learned how to rock and hold. I couldn't take in this reversal of roles.

"You OK, Dad?"

"Yeah, I'll be fine."

"Can I get you anything?"

"No. I'm going for a walk soon," I said, as though I were going to climb Mount Everest. It astounded me how fast my muscles had deteriorated. Five—going on six—days in the hospital, and I was so weak I could barely lift myself out of bed. My muscles were like Jell-O. I'd worked so hard, going to the gym and running in the park, building minuscule quads and abs and triceps, and now they were all gone in a matter of days. "All that work for nothing," I thought. "Why bother?"

"Good morning, Mr. Hamlin."

The respiratory therapist showed up to walk me around the nurses' station. That's as far as I could go. I had to be disconnected from the heart monitor; my breathing tubes needed to be hooked up to a portable tank of oxygen; any medicine that was flowing through the IV would be put on a pole that could come with me. I sat on the side of the bed and looked at my thighs. What thighs? I had none. Sitting up made me woozy. What if I threw up in front of my son?

I smiled to show I was strong, the fake bravery of the patient—"How do you feel today?" "Better. Better." Better on a very low scale. The fevers still came, unpredictable in their arrival, making me wheeze like an old man.

"Let's go for a little walk," said the respiratory therapist.

"Sure."

Sometimes if you act like you feel better, you will feel better. Act like you're hopeful and you *will* feel hopeful, pretend you're happy and maybe you'll feel happy. The emotions normally work from the inside out, but sometimes you can make them work from the outside in. Crack a smile, and it'll warm up your soul, laugh and your spirits will rise. I'd pretended to be well before, maybe I could do it now, indulge in the vast conspiracy of wellness that hospitals unconsciously—or maybe consciously—encourage.

I stood up slowly, the respiratory therapist at my side. Physical and respiratory therapists are the most likable people on earth, paragons of equanimity. I suspect none of them ever had to worry about getting picked to be on a team in junior high school or fretted over what to wear on a first date. They had that kind of inborn confidence. They always acted as if things were fine or would be fine with a little work, no problem. This one was no exception.

"Good," she said with every tentative step I took. "That's very good."

"Where are you ... from?" I asked. I figured if I asked her about herself I wouldn't have to think about how I felt.

Every step forward took enormous effort and concentration. Every joint ached. Every breath was a struggle.

The therapist kept her eye on the oxygen monitor. "Good, good," she said. What was good? Two weeks earlier I had run four miles up and around the park in one of my early morning runs. Now I could barely hobble around the nurses' station. Space had collapsed. My world had shrunk. Goals would be measured in small footsteps, inch by inch.

The therapist was kind and encouraging. "Next time we'll go a little further," she said, walking me back to my room. What I was contending with was the prospect of the long trip I would have to make to get out of the hospital. Distance wasn't just physical, it was emotional. Wellness was so far away. Recovery would be this painful struggle forward every step of the way. There was no magic potion. The doctors were no closer to any reasonable diagnosis. I would have to cling with all my strength to that heaven-sent message: YOU ARE GOING TO GET WELL. God would have to help me because I couldn't do much to help myself. Maybe that needed to be the text of the next e-mail Carol sent: Keep up your prayers, because Rick has just realized how far he has got to go. Perhaps that's what Paul was talking about when he said the Spirit prays for us "in wordless groans." Words were beyond me.

I was escorted back to my bed, exhausted, and discovered that while I was gone, William had made it for me. All those beds we had made for him over the years, the sheets washed, the bedspread tucked in, his stuffed animals piled up in one corner, and now he was making one for me. He sat in the chair, checking messages on his computer, and got up to help. "Thanks," I said. I was grateful. But it also broke my heart.

In the ICU, Carol had taped up opposite my bed a print of two women in 1950s bathing suits doing a circle of flips in an invisible swimming pool, like something from an Esther Williams film. "Rhine maidens," Carol called them. There they were in water portrayed with quick short brushstrokes. "My loop-to-loop girls," was how I thought of them, dancing the light fantastic. They were what I hoped to be, free and fun and floating. They were a prayer and a gift from a friend.

Susan is an artist. I'd seen the original of this print first in her studio in Brooklyn and then in an exhibit framed on a wall. I loved it and told her so. It made me happy. Susan was one of the many who had received Carol's e-mails about my health. She knew I was in dire straits. No visitors yet, but she sent me this copy of her work, e-mailing it to Carol, who had printed it out and put it up. It was my icon, my hope, my wish and belief for myself. My prayer in an image.

You feel so stuck in a hospital room, deprived of all sensory stimulation. The same four walls, the same window, the same tests administered over and over again (blood pressure, temperature, X-ray), the same dull chairs. John Ruskin once said of Constable's paintings when they hung in a gallery that it was as though the wall had been cut open and the sunlight came blazing through. That's how it felt to have Susan's print there, an opening to the world beyond, access to life, beauty, art, love, friends.

Some people ignored the "no visitors" rule or they knew I would have granted them special privileges anyway. Actually, if I'd been the sole gatekeeper, I would have granted hundreds of people special privileges and then felt miserable when I couldn't entertain them. Another failure, another sign of how sick I was. Even when you're a patient and not expected to be at your best, you want to be at your best.

Stacy showed up with her daughter Millie, who I figured was running a race at the Armory next to the hospital.

"How'd it go?"

"Great." Two thumbs-up? Three thumbs-up? I can't remember if Millie won or not, just that she was in her running clothes, and I thought of the times we'd seen her compete at the Armory. But then, the Armory was where they did indoor track in the winter. It wouldn't have made any sense in September. She must have been up in Van Cortlandt Park, one hundred blocks away, and they had stopped by on their way back. It would be like Stacy to act as though they'd just been in the neighborhood. No obligation, nothing special.

They didn't linger. I was grateful for that.

Scott came by. Scott was there a lot. My dearest friend from college, he'd seen me at my best, and plenty of times when I was at my worst. No need to fake it for him. We had more than forty years of friendship through thick and thin, or as another friend likes to say, "May there be more thick than thin." Time for thin.

"What are you doing here?" I asked.

"What are *you* doing here?" he asked.

It's not always easy to visit people in the hospital. You can't just park in front and dart in. Hospitals are also scary for many people, germ-packed petri dishes, harbingers of mortality. Scott came on his way home from work, heading to Westchester from his office on the Upper East Side. Making his way to Washington Heights at rush hour wouldn't be easy. Where did he park? How much did he have to pay?

"That's so nice of you...to come."

"Rick, everybody's been worried about you."

He was there for Carol as much as he was there for me, I told myself. Being a caregiver is not only exhausting, but lonely. Here was a friend to ease the burden, somebody to talk to when I couldn't talk, someone to commiserate with.

"Let me show you...something."

I had been practicing my breathing. I still had the tubes in my nostrils but I had decided that I should always inhale through my nose on a long count and exhale through my mouth. If I did that correctly, breathing would be much easier. If I had to do this the rest of my life with a can of oxygen attached, I would do it. A warm breath of oxygen through the nostrils and deep into my lungs, a smooth exhale of carbon dioxide.

"This is how I'm going to breathe now," I told Carol and Scott. I demonstrated. Scott looked at me like I was nuts, trying to understand, wishing he knew what was on my mind.

"If I can breathe like this, I will be well." I did it again, the tubes of extra oxygen still inserted in my nostrils. Why should breathing right be something so hard? What was I trying to convey?

I saw on Scott's face a look of compassion and bewilderment. I flashed back some forty-odd years to when we were college roommates, and I'd pulled an all-nighter to finish a paper that was due for some class, and I came into our shared dorm room where he was just waking up. He looked at me then, as he did now with love and kindness, and uttered the only thing that made any sense: "You need to get some sleep."

Timothy was leaving for South Africa soon. Friday night his girlfriend Henley had arranged for a surprise good-bye party for him. It would be at our house. I'd somehow fantasized that I would be there too. I'd be in the crowd that burst out "Surprise!" when he came through the door. I'd be able to see some of his old friends, all grown up now. I'd find out what they were doing with themselves.

Carol would go home earlier that night. William would be with her, part of the party. Scott stayed a little while with me, and then I was on my own. "Good-bye, Tim. It must be a sign that I'm getting better, or you wouldn't feel you could leave. I'm not there, but I'm always there. Dads are always there. It's just the way things work out. I hope—I pray—that I'm there for the good, that I'm some sort of inner voice that says, 'You're gifted, you're loved, you're a delight, you're all a dad would ever hope for.' You are. Love, Dad."

Sept. 18, 4:19 p.m.

I am not at the hospital.

Just think about that for a moment, friends. Sunny, warm September afternoon and I am at my desk, looking at the Hudson. For that matter, Rick is not even in his hospital bed, I'm told: word from Will is "they took him down for a sonogram."

This would have been incredibly cumbersome yesterday, tethered as he has been to his blood pressure cuff and his EKG sensors and his utterly essential 02 machine. But this morning they took him off the high-flow machine and gave him one of those little cannula things: the prongs you stick in your nose, attached to a clear hose, attached to heaven knows what and a green-painted tank. And two respiratory therapists walked him around the halls with his two tanks of 02 in a little truncated cart, and he was stepping out briskly.

There is even talk of moving to a "quieter room," which probably means off the step-down ward, and while we will miss the remarkable people there, quiet would be good.

Today's diagnosis hypothesis is a kind of squishy combo thing: underlying immune disorder, which produced alarming symptoms when prodded into action by unidentified viral infection. Whatever. Sounds as if there may be more tests later, once Rick's lungs have healed further.

There is even talk of Rick being able to take a shower. Just imagine what that will feel like after a week in a hospital bed.

Love to you all, C.

CHAPTER EIGHT

Hospital, Day 6

Have you ever worked in a shipyard?"
"Have you traveled abroad recently?"
"How long ago was it that you were in Africa?"
"Do you have any exotic birds?"
"Do you have any pets?"
"Have you been in the Central Valley?"
"Do you have any allergies?"

One question that no doctor ever asked was, "Have you ever suffered from depression?"

It wouldn't have been there in my chart. You couldn't find it in the digital records that Columbia-Presbyterian was so proud to keep, that information any professional affiliated with the hospital could find at the click of a key. Did anyone ever think to ask it? I never thought to say it. And what if they'd asked, and what if I'd said yes... would it have made any difference in the diagnosis they were trying to put together?

"Yes," I could say, "I've been battling depression for over a year now, maybe a year and a half."

"Really?"

"I've been seeing a therapist."

"Any meds?"

"No. It doesn't feel like that kind of depression. I don't object to antidepressants, although I've never had them.

I wouldn't hesitate to take them if they were prescribed. They never have been."

If I'd been on meds, it would have been in my records, right?

"I've been treating this with talk therapy. Funny thing: it was all winding down before this infection hit me. In fact, my last appointment with the shrink was scheduled for the week I got sick."

"Your last appointment?"

"My last for a while. My friend Rick, who is a therapist, has this nice phrase, 'You don't ever stop therapy,' he says. 'You simply take a break from it.' I was at that point and had told the therapist, 'I'm ready to take a break.' Then came this."

"Why do you bring it up?"

"It obviously had some effect on my immune system."

I'm usually more prone to anxiety than depression, forging ahead with nervous anticipation rather than gazing behind in numbing regret. "Feigning frenzy" was how Scott described it in our college days, whether it was feigned or not.

Then, about a year before I landed in the hospital, the veil started to descend. Everything seemed dark, my reactions fearful. On an August weekend in Martha's Vineyard with dear friends, I woke up to sunlight streaming into our bedroom, the curtains billowing in the breeze. Logically I knew the day was something to be enjoyed—beautiful weather, warm ocean water for swimming, the chance to lounge on a porch swing with a good book, the prospect of reminiscing with old friends. Instead I dreaded it. I looked at the clear blue sky with horror. I didn't want to talk to anyone. Didn't want to meet any new people—a rare state for an extrovert like me. First thing in the morning I went for a run to be on my own. Later, when we went swimming, I found myself drifting with the current, glad to be taken away from the group. "How far out could I go without being noticed?" I wondered. At dinner that night, sitting with people I loved, I found myself counting the minutes, glancing at my watch, wondering how soon I could politely say, "Gosh, it's so late. I think I need to go to bed."

I could still make conversation, lobbing questions back and forth, appearing to be interested in all that was said. I could smile and laugh, but it was someone else doing it, not me. Echoing the psalmist, I prayed, "Why are you cast down O my soul, and why are you disquieted within me?" How could I be such a stranger to myself?

I came to be obsessed with death that summer. Any life span I saw, the years attached to historical personages like, say, George Washington (1732–1799), Thomas Jefferson (1743–1826), or Theodore Roosevelt (1858–1919), got me thinking how long I had lived and could possibly live, measuring my life against theirs. *Lord, teach us to number our days so that we may gain a heart to wisdom.* "George Washington didn't even make it to seventy," I thought. "Teddy Roosevelt was only a year older than

109

me when he died." Instead of looking to the future with wonder and hope, imagining all the things I could and would do, I saw it with blinders. Life didn't feel like a gift anymore. I started writing about all the guys I'd known back in the eighties and nineties, guys my age, who had died from AIDS. Their loss seemed even sadder now than it had then. All the things they had missed. "Borrowed Time" I wanted to call it, although that title was already taken by an AIDS memoir. Didn't we all live on borrowed time?

On Martha's Vineyard I was determined to find the grave site of the first Hamlin to come to these shores, back in the seventeenth century. A kindly *Guideposts* reader with the same last name, who turned out to be a distant cousin, had sent me a notebook outlining our shared genealogy. He pointed out that our ancestor James Hamlin (1636–1718) was buried in a cemetery in the middle of the island. I hitched a ride to the spot, convinced that his tombstone would be impossible to find, buried under brambles. But no, I found it in minutes and gazed with fascination at the winged skull on the tombstone, taking some sort of comfort in the image of death wearing angel wings. I recalled an octogenarian friend who, in considering death, said she prayed for a "direct flight." Seemed like a good idea.

That August, when most New York psychotherapists decamp to Wellfleet or Woodstock, I found one who was still in town. I met with her every Friday at one o'clock, taking a subway to the Upper East Side from our offices down in the Financial District. There were days I didn't like to stand too close to the edge of the platform, too close to the oncoming train.

"I wouldn't ever commit suicide," I told my shrink, "but I understand now why people do it." I could see what a relief it would be, an escape from the grayness inside, death an odd sort of blessing. Was it possible that depression was a way for us to prepare for death, to learn how to let go? Was I being asked to make better friends with death, to see it as part of the natural cycle of life?

I could look at myself from the outside and seem so normal, nothing apparently wrong. I went running or hauled myself to the gym six days a week (taking an exercise Sabbath on Sundays). I went to the office, edited stories, sat through meetings. Sang in choir, organized a church men's group that met once a month to talk about our concerns and pray for one another. I wasn't shy about sharing my own gloomy state and asking for prayers. I continued my own private prayer practice, stretching the time. Closing my eyes, I would sit on the sofa cross-legged and sink into silent meditation, checking out to check in, trying to let go of all the worries that clouded my head. I rose from the couch, the gloom still there.

I believed that this dark patch, this psychic disconnect, was meant to teach me something—good Puritan soul that I am—and I would ask myself and ask the therapist a million questions to understand why and how I'd gotten here. I'd been in therapy before, had put a few bogeymen to rest. By and large my childhood had been happy. I was loved in a family that is still very close. I could look back and find a few untoward moments of unhappiness, but they felt well explored, talked about in previous therapy sessions. Relinquished. The wounds didn't seem worth picking at anymore. Why this now? What was happening to me? It was affecting my body as well as my soul.

"It feels like some lingering PTSD from open-heart surgery," I proposed to the shrink.

"Let's talk about that," she said.

Dear reader, forgive me for going into this now, another organ recital at this late juncture in this reminiscence that is already overcrowded with medical detail. I've hinted enough at it and talked around it, thinking I wouldn't have to explain too much. It was there in my medical records for all to see. "Bovine valve...aortic root replacement." But when I talk about depression I have to talk about this, the surgery I'd had at the same hospital, Columbia-Presbyterian, eight years earlier.

I was born with a bicuspid aortic valve and developed an aortic aneurysm at age fifty-two. As my cardiac surgeon explained, "If you have a bicuspid valve you've got a fifty-fifty chance of getting an aneurysm." Thanks to my pulmonologist, Dr. DiMango, as I've mentioned, the problem was discovered. She'd asked me to have an MRI for reasons that had nothing to do with my heart and then called me and said, in her memorable words, "Your lungs are fine, but you'd better do something about that aneurysm in your aorta."

I met with Beloved Cardiologist Dr. Ravalli on a Thursday. This was when we had talked about Italy for twenty minutes before he'd delivered the news, "You're going to need open-heart surgery." Carol and I met the cardiac surgeon the following Monday—"Doctor God" she'd dubbed him. I had checked into the hospital that Wednesday and had surgery the next day, December 7, Pearl Harbor Day.

I didn't expect surgery to be a picnic, but nothing had prepared me for how brutal recovery would be. I was healthy, in good shape. I'd had no symptoms (which, upon reflection, was less than comforting). Doctor God spoke euphemistically about the operation and how smooth it would be. "We'll stretch open the sternum," he said. Stretch open? *Saw open* would be more accurate. "It should be a six-hour operation," he said. Six hours? The anesthesiologist put me out at around one o'clock in the afternoon and I didn't wake up in the ICU until after one in the morning, with a nurse named Angel, I kid you not, hovering over me.

"We were planning to go on a trip to Spain after the holidays," we told Doctor God.

"No problem," he said. "I'll fix you up, and then you can go on and live your life."

My body ached, not just my chest but my back and

shoulders. They get you up and walking as soon as possible after heart surgery, but I didn't want to go anywhere. I was in the hospital recovering for six days, then came home and recovered for six weeks, never taking naps, walking a bit and then walking a bit more.

I'd heard enough about how depression was often a result of open-heart surgery, but I wouldn't describe what I felt then as depression. I was tired but I couldn't fall asleep at night. It was as though my body were saying, "Don't you check out on me. Remember what happened when they put you out in the OR? Remember what they did to you? Sawed open your chest, hooked you up to the heart-lung machine while you were really dead?" I was eternally wary. The gremlins had attacked once. Maybe they would attack again.

We did not go to Spain.

I described all this to my psychotherapist, reliving it to try to understand it, looking under psychic bedcovers to see if the unacknowledged trauma of open-heart surgery— one of those things that people don't talk about—had led somehow to depression now, eight years later.

I would tell her how wired I was, on edge, for weeks after the surgery. I was like a dog during a thunderstorm, desperate to be around people, wanting to be told that everything was going to be all right. My heart would race at ninety beats a minute on my way to cardiac rehab. "It must be the coffee you have at breakfast," Dr. Ravalli said. "I don't drink coffee," I said. "It's probably your heart anticipating the workout you're going to get at cardiac rehab," he said, ever reassuring.

I remember running into neighbors as I was making my way to the deli or the cleaner's, trying to get some exercise. "What happened to you?" the more honest ones could say. I would explain and tell them about the aortic aneurysm and the surgery that Doctor God had performed. "Well, you look great," one woman said. "Thanks," I said. I saw her a couple of weeks later. "You look so much better now," she said. "You looked terrible last time I saw you. I thought you were at death's door."

Never trust what anyone says to you when you're recovering from illness.

The worst symptom was something I came to call "the black domino," a darkness inside my head. It was especially pronounced when I tried to pray. I would close my eyes to sink into what I hoped would be a healing meditation and instead find myself tumbling down a dark hole. It was as though part of my brain had been blasted out of my head, leaving nothing but pitch black. I could almost locate it, toward the top of my brain.

"Why did you call it the black domino?" my therapist asked.

"I don't know." My brain danced to make connections like you do in a therapist's office. "It just seemed like solid darkness, like a black domino if you broke it up inside. Or maybe it's the way you line them up and push one, and they all fall down."

"Is it still there?"

"It lifted after several months, was gone in a year. But if I think about it long enough, I can still feel where it was." I closed my eyes. I didn't want to find it, didn't like facing it, but maybe that's why I needed to face it. "Right there." My place of comfort had been hijacked, and it made me mad and scared me to death.

A year of talking to the psychotherapist, a year of dragging myself up to her office on East Eighty-Sixth Street and sitting there, digging deep, dumping, dredging up what needed to be dredged. Did I like doing it? Not really. Did I resent the time it took out of my day? Yeah, until I considered how much more time I had wasted by burying things. Did I resent the money it cost? Terribly. Did I think it was necessary? Absolutely. The depression eased, glimpses of light started casting themselves into the gloom, I was mending. I was ready to take a break. And now this.

Why hadn't any doctor asked if I'd been depressed? Surely it had weakened my immune system. Maybe it had made me vulnerable to infection. Wasn't that something the docs would want to know? But then, it wasn't something I wanted to talk about.

Even now.

They were moving me out of the ICU step-down into a shared room at the end of the hall, from Garden South to Garden North. They were lowering my dose of oxygen, they were finishing up the round of antibiotics. I was getting better—all signs pointed that way—but I was only feeling worse. "If this is better," I thought, "I don't like it."

The doctors came around, ordering more tests and then waiting to find out what the tests would say. The specialists arrived with different troops of residents or students, and I would be exhibit A. Don't get me wrong, I was glad of the attention. Whatever I could do to help. If they could only come up with a diagnosis.

I hated saying good-bye to my favorite nurse, Jay, even though he was just down the hall. The shower he had promised would have to wait for someone else to administer it. I dreaded leaving one cocoon of care for another and disliked being so sensitive about it. I hated how a fever could still leave me gasping for breath. How was I ever going to get back to normal?

Trust, trust, trust, trust, I preached to myself. Carol printed out some of the e-mails, and I managed to read them, good wishes from people thinking about me, worried about me, praying for me. *You are loved, Rick,* I told myself. *Feel it. Trust it. Know it.*

Soon William would go back to San Francisco. Soon Timothy would leave for South Africa. Oh, how I'd miss them. "The next time you see your father I won't look like this, I promise. I will be OK." *Receive the love, Rick.*

September 19, 8:27 p.m.
    The paradox of recovery: sometimes it's not until you feel better that you actually feel sick.

Are you with me? The docs moved Rick from the step-down unit (as in a "step down" from the ICU) to a general medicine ward, thereby releasing/removing him from lots of systemic support and monitoring. Which is progress. But now that he's not getting as much oxygen and not being checked on hourly etc. etc. he feels, as his mother would say, "pretty punk." Me, I see this as the bumpy road to eventual health. But he did spike a fever this morning and has to work harder to breathe. Plus the poor guy never got his shower.

And let's be realistic: this drama has lasted a full week now. We're all bored and tired, Rick most of all.

We've got personnel changes over the next couple of days. Will returns to SF, Tim heads off to SA (that would be South Africa), and Rick's brother Howard joins the support team here. I will admit that I am exhausted but I am fortified by the generosity and inventive concern of neighbors and friends. I come home: there is strange and wonderful food in my fridge. How cool is that?

We are not out of the woods but I have to believe that all these prayers and loving thoughts are making a difference.

XXX, C.

CHAPTER NINE

Hospital, Days 7 and 8

We faith people, we tell ourselves stories, retell them, then tell them again. It's gone on that way for millennia. They remind us of who we are and whose we are. Lost in my hospital bed, I looked for signs that what I believed to be true would be true. That this misery and boredom would have some purpose. My body was giving me conflicting messages. My soul wanted to trust in better news.

"Remember how much you worried about Tim? Remember how hard you and Carol prayed? Look how that turned out. Isn't there some lesson you can hold on to now?"

You worry about your grown-up kids as they head into the world. You think you know what's best for them. You want to show them the way. You want to engineer a future for them. And make it happen right away. If you could, you would wave a magic wand that would open all the right doors, even if that would rob them of the necessary learning experiences—terrible notion—that make for a magna cum laude in the School of Hard Knocks. Short of that, you make suggestions, you send links to helpful articles (my dad sent clippings), you make phone calls, you mention that you know someone who would love to talk to them and might have just the right idea for them, knowing as you do that sometimes someone who isn't Dad might be able to get through.

To watch William make the transition from college to career was relatively easy. But then, he was an econ major. The way was paved with campus visits from recruiters who were only too glad to sign up a numbers guy with social skills. He had a job offer before he graduated and took it. Happily.

It's harder, though, for a humanities graduate to determine what the away-from-academia future holds. I should know. I graduated from college determined not to sign on the dotted line of any program designed to turn an English major into an investment banker or stockbroker or even a schoolteacher. I didn't want to have a salaried job for years—and didn't. As I mentioned, I went off to Italy and then did theater and freelance writing. But what do you do when you see your history major son look with bewilderment at the choices after graduation?

"Come home," we told Tim. "You can live with us till you figure something out. You've got loads of talent. There are tons of things you can do. Something great will turn up."

You want to be a blindly encouraging parent while offering occasional doses of practicality, bits of solid advice. Tim seemed so disheartened I didn't even dare do that. The merest hint of a suggestion, and he closed down.

I didn't bring up any mention of faith or prayer or church. Both of our boys had grown up going to church every Sunday, a nonnegotiable. They attended Sunday school—for a couple of years I was their teacher. Timothy sang in church choirs from the time he was four years old to his senior year of high school. I was aware that his faith had lapsed in college, but that didn't seem unusual. I'd had my own flirtation with atheism in college until the urgency of final exams and the lure of the Princeton University Chapel changed all that. You lose your parents' faith so that you can find a faith of your own. To pray that Tim found his way back to God seemed beyond hoping. It was painful enough to watch him struggle with day-to-day life in the real world.

I felt like I had to tiptoe around him, vacillating between telling him exactly what he should do and keeping my mouth shut for fear I'd destroy any shred of confidence he had. In my prayers I went through a litany of things that God was supposed to do for him. "He'd be a great teacher. He should look into that…He's a fine musician. He should start a rock band…God, have you seen what a superb writer he is? Don't you think he should do something with that? We've got tons of friends in nonprofits—I want him to talk to all of them. Lord, tell him he needs to listen to me and follow my advice."

As fellow blogger Julia Attaway recently reminded me, "Let go and let God" is about *not* dictating but accepting.

Tim found immediate employment as a babysitter, a "manny" in contemporary parlance. He is very good with children, has endless patience, and kids naturally glom on to him. He was hired to pick up a sixth-grader from school a couple of days a week, supervising homework and taking the boy to after-school music lessons and karate. He had another gig for a young family so the mom and dad could have a marriage-saving date night. He was employed by one couple who had adopted a boy from Ethiopia and another couple with two boys who needed an agile referee.

He worked all year taking care of kids. His only immediate goal was to put aside enough money to see more of the world. Wanderlust? I understood that. After all, what did I do when I was his age? Expatriated to Florence. But surely I had more focus back then—didn't I?—more drive, clearer goals. I was going to be a writer or a singer or a citizen of the world. Something like that. "Tim, perhaps you should...," I'd start to suggest, stopping myself at a kick from Carol under the table to zip it, Dad.

By June Tim had enough saved to see the world with a friend for as long as the money would hold out. We wished him bon voyage. The e-mails came from Spain, France, Morocco, Italy, Croatia, Bosnia, Jordan, Israel, Egypt, India. Curiously enough I worried less about him when he was on the road, even when he was in places noted for political unrest.

He and his buddy spent one week on a beach on the Sinai Peninsula, taking care not to reveal where they were until after they'd left, saving us the worries, unless we wanted to worry about things that had already passed, which is always a possibility. By November they were wrapping up five weeks of third-class rail travel through India, with a few too many nights sleeping in train stations, when I got the e-mail that stopped me in my tracks.

He'd been at shrines that attracted pilgrims from all over the country, Hindus and Moslems practicing their faith. "It's pretty interesting," he wrote, "but it makes me think I should learn more about what I grew up with. I need to understand Christianity better. Is there an Episcopal monastery back in New York where I could spend some time, learning about my faith?"

Wow. Where did that come from? It was certainly never a directive in my prayers. I'm not that clever.

"Sure, Tim," I wrote back, my fingers flying across the keys. "There are some Episcopal brothers who have a monastery up the Hudson somewhere. I'll find the name of it. We know lots of people who've gone there on retreats." There it was online, "Holy Cross Monastery, an Anglican Benedictine Community of Men." I got the snail mail address and the name of the prior.

Timothy came home in late November, wrote a letter to the prior, and on a cold January day he took the train up to Poughkeepsie, got a cab to go across the river, and spent a couple of days with the good brothers at Holy Cross. "Come back and stay longer," they said. He did, spending six weeks with them, reading, praying, saying the monastic offices, sledding on a snow day, doing a little work in the kitchen. It was a transforming experience. He'd never been so happy in his life. They didn't charge him. They welcomed him in the age-old Benedictine tradition of hospitality, taking in the stranger as though he were Christ himself. Tim found his faith. Born again. He came back to New York with a new focus, an inner direction.

He became active in our church, the church where he had grown up. Every Friday he'd work to prepare whatever was being cooked for Saturday's soup kitchen and he'd serve the meal on Saturdays, no matter how late he stayed out on Friday nights with his pals. He volunteered one night a week at a homeless shelter. He read, he worshipped, trying to figure out what he wanted to do next. Seminary maybe, possibly the ministry. He applied for a program called "Young Adult Service Corps" that ended up sending him for ten months to South Africa. There he would be living with the Holy Cross brothers, the same group of men who'd brought him to this new spiritual home.

It was nothing I had dreamed up, nothing I had engineered. I couldn't have come up with something this good. I would have done better by trusting God than wasting my energy telling Him what to do.

Trust, trust, trust.

I had a roommate in my new room, an older man without much English. I couldn't get much out of him and was relieved that he didn't watch much TV. He was obviously afraid and he wouldn't cooperate with the nurses, wouldn't eat the food. When he was scheduled for a test—a CT scan or echocardiogram—he refused to go. He was terribly alone. Unlike me, he had no visitors. Every day he'd get a phone call from someone and yell into the phone. He was fiercely unhappy, and no one could seem to do anything about it. I admired the way the nurses treated him. They never lost their patience. I tried to talk to him but we had little language in common. I nodded and smiled on my way to the john when I passed his bed.

"I'm sorry that we have made so much noise," I said. Carol had been there, Scott came, someone from church came. He nodded. That was it.

I wanted to see this new room as an exit ramp. I had been given my internal marching orders—I was going to get out of here—but they didn't come with any date stamped on them. How much longer would I be in the hospital? When would I finally get out? When would the fevers leave? When would I get off the oxygen?

I felt well enough to know how rotten I was. I was getting enough good news to know how very bad the news had been, getting enough glimpses of light to feel the contrasting dark. I could finally prop myself up with my laptop and read messages sent to me, warming, loving notes of prayer and concern, but I didn't have enough energy to respond. I didn't have the wherewithal to organize the messages in any fashion, forgetting which ones to mark "read" or "unread." I guess this is where the term "executive function" comes in. I had lost mine.

This was the week I was supposed to be in California for that conference. I wanted to let my colleagues know I was thinking of them, but I didn't trust my ability to come up with a decent message. Odd self-consciousness for someone who never hesitates before sending a message to anyone. The blank page had never seemed like an enemy before. Now it was intimidating.

For the first time I logged on to Facebook and posted something:

September 20.

Dear friends, I am now entering my second week at Columbia-Presbyterian Hospital, being treated for a rather baffling lung infection. The staff is superb, and I certainly feel better today than I did a week ago, but fevers persist and my breathing is halting at best. I can't tell you how grateful I am for your prayers, because they seem to tide me over when fatigue makes it hard for me to pray. Keep 'em coming. Forgive me for not responding individually to your kind wishes. I am confident in my doctors and confident in my own faith. I grow weary, I confess, but I do not despair. Godspeed.

I am still amazed at how many people that update reached, more than anything I've ever posted before. The number of comments was astounding, comments I could barely take in. All those people: friends, family, readers, strangers, friends of friends. Bad news travels fast.

I was reading Tolkien's magisterial *The Lord of the Rings*. I had bought a copy for my Kindle not long before I landed in the hospital, the trilogy in a single volume.

I'd tried to tackle it before when the boys were very young. I had a paperback edition of *The Fellowship of the Ring*, and was reading it on the subway home from work back in the days when New York was not as safe a city as it is today.

It was rush hour. I was on the A train, rumbling under Harlem, the book in my lap. I guess I closed my eyes for a moment, maybe in prayer, maybe in sleep. The next thing I knew some troubled fellow traveler was slugging me in the face for no apparent reason. I ducked my head—didn't ever see him—and darted off the train, carrying my bloodstained book. I wasn't hurt badly but I didn't have any appetite to continue with Tolkien.

Now I'd gone back to it, the stirring drama of good versus evil taking me away from my own shapeless narrative of hospitalization. I once wrote a novel about a dying woman who communicates with her husband from beyond the grave through a series of messages she scrawled in the margins of one of her favorite paperback books, a novel she knew he'd discover at some point after her death. *Reading between the Lines*, I called it.

Reading between the lines of Tolkien, I highlighted passages on my Kindle that spoke to me:

There is a seed of courage hidden (often deeply, it is true) in the heart of the fattest and most timid hobbit, waiting for some final and desperate danger to make it grow.

Where was my seed of courage?

"Despair or folly?" said Gandalf. "It is not despair, for despair is only for those who see the end beyond all doubt. We do not."

What was the end of this?

Sam said nothing. The look on Frodo's face was enough for him; he knew that words of his were useless. And after all he never had any real hope in the affair from the beginning; but being a cheerful hobbit he had not needed hope, as long as despair could be postponed. Now they were come to the bitter end. But he had stuck to his master all the way; that was what he had chiefly come for, and he would still stick to him. His master would not go to Mordor alone. Sam would go with him—and at any rate they would get rid of Gollum.

Or get rid of mysterious, life-threatening, impossible-to-diagnose lung infections.

Sept. 20, 2:36 p.m.
    Dear friends, I'm thinking the narrative drive of this story is starting to sag. There isn't much I can do about the real-time aspect of our drama, so I'm going to

Space

It

Out.

That is to say, communicate less often. So don't freak out—or assume that he's home in his own bed—when you don't hear from me tomorrow. Chances are excellent the status will be quo.

Rick is improving for sure. He did get that shower today and has tottered around the room on his long O2 hose. Less happily he spiked fevers both yesterday and today, so we got a return visit this afternoon from the chief of the rheumatology department, who seemed intent on further diagnostic activity. Not that I can imagine what that would be. I'm getting a faint whiff of "Groundhog Day" here.

Our patient is still not ready for visitors, though I know many of you are very eager. His energy is too limited to make his responding to e-mails a sure bet. So keep us in your thoughts and prayers, and don't get alarmed when there's no bulletin tomorrow.

Lots of love from the entire Hamlin family, C.

CHAPTER TEN

Hospital, Days 9 and 10

T hen the most extraordinary thing happened, a gift that came out of the blue. Maybe this is what people mean when they talk about the blessings to be found in the midst of suffering, how reservoirs of goodness and kindness reveal themselves, how joy tumbles out from the clouds.

Howard wasn't really lurking in the clouds. He was in Annapolis, Maryland, competing in a regatta.

Howard is my older brother and a world-class competitive sailor. For nearly forty years he's been racing 505's and other demanding sailboats.

Sailing is supposed to be mind-numbingly boring as a spectator sport. "Like watching grass grow," they say. Not Howard's kind of sailing. I watched him race off the Denmark coast when we were in our twenties and again off Cape Cod when we were in our forties, and more recently back in California when he was in his early sixties, as he is now. Nobody races his sorts of boats at our age. It takes too much stamina, fortitude, muscle power, endurance. It's just too hard. Not for Howard. He flies down to Australia every winter—their summer—to race skiffs in Sydney Harbour, and then competes in another regatta on Lake Garda in Italy or off the coast of France, practicing in the waters back home in Southern California.

These boats go so fast they are more likely to tip end over end, tripping over a wave bow first, like a kid doing a cartwheel, rather than tip over on their side (guess what a mess that would make of the rigging).

Howard has brought those same speed-racing skiffs to San Francisco Bay for a regatta every year, where spectators can watch the boats plane across the water, racing under the Golden Gate and past Alcatraz. I love the photos of Howard—or Howie, as his fellow sailors call him—hiking so far out in his wet suit that only his toes touch the edge of the boat, his body parallel to the bay. Imagine the sort of strength it takes to do that well or how much pummeling your joints absorb over the years, your knees like rubber bands. It's certainly taken its toll on his body. He doesn't go out of the house without doing forty-five minutes of stretches and exercises every morning. That's what it takes to keep him vertical.

In our family we joke about Howard's high pain threshold and his tireless athleticism. We like to repeat his once-made claim: "If I don't sail or surf or ski I'll develop lower back pain within twenty-four hours" ("Hey, Howard, for most of us it's the other way around"), or we remember the time he told his wife, Julie, after she suggested that maybe they didn't need to drive up to the Sierras to ski for the umpteenth weekend in a row: "Julie, if we don't go this weekend, it'll be lost. You can't make it up." *You can't make it up.* You can't. One time he broke his pelvis skiing in the

Sierras and still hobbled on board his flight home, walking into his doctor's office the next day. "You shouldn't even be standing," the doctor declared after studying the X-ray.

Howard has a small real-estate business with an office in Huntington Beach, close enough to the beach so that he can surf for an hour before work. This is his meditation time, as essential to him as my sitting on the couch every morning with my eyes closed. He stares at the incoming waves, sizing them up in the wind or fog, riding the right one, getting connected with God's creation.

Howard was sailing on the East Coast when I landed in the hospital, competing in the North American championship of 505's. He e-mailed Carol and said, "I want to talk."

She called him from the garden courtyard of the hospital, outside when she was taking a break. Howard wanted to know exactly what was going on, and Carol spelled it out, straightforward. "OK," he said, "I'm coming to help out." He didn't ask, he told her. It was a done deal.

He won the North Americans in Annapolis, as he's won the title seven times before, more than anyone else—something that didn't register with me till many months later—and then he flew up to be with us in New York. I don't know what he did with his boat or what sort of penalty he had to pay to change his flight. He just appeared.

On Monday he walked into my hospital room. "Hey, Howie," I said.

"Hey. How are you?"

"Not great." Pause. "But getting better. I'm getting better."

"Good."

That's the world Howard lives in, akin to the world we were raised in, one of abiding optimism, an inheritance from our parents, especially our sunny-tempered mom. Things are always meant to get better. Hope was in the smoggy, sunburned Southern California air we breathed.

Howard sat by my bed for three days, relieving Carol of that duty so she could unwind in the gym at least once or twice and not rush to my bedside at the crack of dawn. He could take in what the doctors were saying, ask questions about what tests they wanted to give me, write down notes on what they said and share it with Carol.

But he also just sat there. He was probably doing some work on his computer or phone, in between the doctor visits. It might sound counterintuitive that an adrenaline junkie like Howard could be so good at sitting, but he is. I was reminded of how he sat by our father's bed, holding Dad's hand for hours, when Dad was dying. I needed to get up and move around. Howard could just sit.

It took me back to our childhood, all those years that Howard and I had shared a bedroom.

That room was a converted garage, the sliding glass doors opening up to the driveway, convenient for sneaking out at night. We could go upstairs and tell Mom and Dad, "I'm home," and then go right back out without having to escape through some upstairs window. Howard could also bring in his minibikes and go-cart for the night, the faint whiff of gasoline the room's abiding scent. His bed was next to an old rolltop desk, and mine next to an upright piano with tacks on the hammers so it gave a honky-tonk tone when I played "Maple Leaf Rag."

I remember him sitting up in that bed in the early morning of a February day in 1971 when the Sylmar earthquake rattled the Southland, rumbling underground like a roadster, rousing us from sleep.

"Bitchin'," he said. "An earthquake!"

(*Bitchin'* was surfer slang for "cool" or "neat" or "far out.")

A disaster was not to be dreaded but celebrated, a break in the norm, maybe offering up the possibility of canceled classes like snow days, something not regularly afforded Southern Californians.

He was right in his hope that school would be canceled for the day, but for some reason afternoon rehearsals for the high school musical were not. I was in the musical; he was not.

We were as different as two brothers could be. Howard was risk taking and physical; mechanically adept, he never met a gadget he didn't want to take apart. I was bookish and musical, memorizing the lyrics to every original Broadway cast album I could buy.

As a kid he liked building forts in the back forty and digging deep holes for lighting bonfires. I stood by with a cupful of water as though I could halt the blaze if any sparks flew. I put on plays in the backyard, casting the neighbors in productions of "Rumpelstiltskin" and "Snow White," the Seven Dwarves singing "Heigh-ho, heigh-ho" as they marched down through the camellias from their "mines" up by Howard's tree house. He wouldn't have considered taking a role in my amateur productions—nor would I have asked—but he made a curtain that could actually be raised and lowered in the gazebo we used for our stage, a foreshadowing of his talent for rigging sailboats.

We talked at night before going to bed, staring up at the gray ceiling. When he fell madly in love in high school—more than once—he'd sneak out that sliding glass door and then return later, exclaiming to his younger brother, "You don't know what it's like." I would find out.

We would enshrine our loved ones' front yard with streams of toilet paper, fluttering from bushes and trees as a sign of our not-so-secret devotion. Getting "t.p.-ed" was a singular honor. One night I was privileged to join Howard on such an escapade, dodging a cop car, running away from a father's flashlight. How to explain the allure of a roll of t.p. shooting through the branches of an oak tree in the lamplight, leaving a streak of white tail, then landing in the grass with a dull thud? Those thuds were something you listened for as you hurled the toilet paper into the trees. I could still hear them now in a hospital bed, taking comfort in the memory of a less dangerous time.

No, that's not fair. There were all sorts of dangers back then, the risk of having your heart broken (what if the girl didn't want to be t.p.-ed?), the real possibility that you'd humiliate yourself in the high school musical, the potential for the next earthquake to be ten times worse, bringing down the house around you.

"That reminds me," I wanted to say. I wanted to retell my favorite Howard story from childhood. There was no need to, of course. He knew the story; I knew it. And he knows how funny I think it is, how it cracks me up every time I tell it. But we didn't have to talk. We could just be with each other. The best hospital visitor is someone who doesn't need much talking, who doesn't require any entertaining, and yet you can say to him or her a thousand things in silence, and they'll get every word.

Of all the backyard forts Howard built, the most elaborate had an elevator that was meant to take you to the third or fourth floor. The whole thing was a rickety concoction of refrigerator boxes (where did we get those?), old fencing, two-by-fours, and plywood sheets, a recycled lumberyard. It probably wasn't the skyscraper it is in my mind's eye. It couldn't have been more than eight or nine feet tall (it was probably less) because it would have towered over the back fence, calling for an inspection from the fire marshal. In fact, I don't know why Mom and Dad never saw it or came to tear it down. Maybe because they were busy enough with the four of us kids, all two years apart. Maybe because one of the best gifts they gave us in a pre-"helicopter parent" era was to love us by leaving us alone.

Upon completion of this masterpiece Howard wanted

to get the elevator to work and he wanted to be the first one to ride it to the top floor. The elevator car was basically a crate with a rope attached, thrown over a beam at the top of the fort.

"Pull," Howard said. He sat in the box, and I pulled the rope. The crate didn't budge.

"Pull harder," Howard said. I pulled with all my strength. Nothing.

He went over to our next door neighbor's house and grabbed a cohort. The two of us pulled. We jiggled the crate a little bit, but we still weren't strong enough to raise it all the way. We needed more manpower. Howard knocked on more doors and got some more willing accomplices. We gathered around the rope. "Pull!" he shouted to all of us. We grabbed hold and pulled and pulled and pulled. Howard rose slowly in the air, the elevator bumping against his skyscraper. He smiled triumphantly at us, the builder enjoying the view.

He finally reached the top and sat there in the crate for a moment, the lord of all he surveyed. Just then the fort wobbled a bit, and then wobbled some more. "Hold on to the rope," Howard said.

We held on to the rope.

But we couldn't stop the shaking. Walls ballooned out, beams started bending, there was a cracking sound, some flimsy boards breaking, and then a terrible shuddering. Sawdust flew in the air, refrigerator cardboard crumbled. The whole Tower of Babel came crashing down, the rope flying through our fingers, Howard plummeting to the earth, his fort landing around him and on top of him.

We scrambled out of the way and then raced back, lifting up boards and two-by-fours, searching for Howard, fearing the worst, certain to find his corpse. I don't think he was older than fourth or fifth grade, which would have put me in first or second. He'd already broken his arm once by then, and had had his tonsils taken out, and had to be taken in an ambulance from school when he'd fallen on his throat, jumping from bench to bench in the playground, almost strangling himself. What would an ambulance do now when they came to pick him up? What could they do with a dead body?

We finally dug him out and came upon him sitting on the ground with the crate on top of him, the rope at his feet. But he wasn't dead at all. He was laughing, laughing so hard he couldn't stop.

"Howard, you could have killed yourself," one of the older, wiser neighborhood boys said.

"But I didn't," he said, still laughing. That was Howard, the miracle kid, walking away from disaster, laughing.

I could still see that look on his face when the fort was starting to tremble, and all of us were clutching that rope. Sheer terror. And yet he'd survived.

Yes, Rick, you will get out of here. Yes, Rick, you will get well. No, that notion you had of getting better, that wasn't just a phantom. That promise was real. You feel rotten right now, and breathing is still hard when you run a fever, but it won't always be that way. Look how far you've come already. Look at the progress you've made. I couldn't hold on to that promise without help.

"For I was hungry and you gave me food, I was thirsty and you gave me something to drink, I was a stranger and you welcomed me, I was naked and you gave me clothing, I was sick and you cared for me…," Jesus said. That is the gift of the hospital visitor, to give your true self back to you. Howard, Carol, the boys, Scott—they all did that.

"I was sick and you visited me." Those words were on a plaque outside the care facility where my father died, where Howard had sat by that bed for hours.

Both Howard and Carol were there to hear an exchange between two of my doctors.

First there was the arrival of an older specialist I had never met, white-haired and distinguished looking even in his untailored white coat. He had a team of younger fellows with him, and I was, evidently, exhibit X, to be poked and prodded and questioned. They were standing at the head of my bed, beginning their inspection, when at the foot of my bed Dr. Ravalli arrived, my beloved Italian cardiologist. Apparently they knew each other.

"Hello," Dr. Ravalli said.

"Hi, babe," said the distinguished-looking specialist.

Hi, babe? Did he really say that? All three of us heard it, "babe," about as politically incorrect a nomenclature as can be, except, I suppose, when given to another man of the same age.

Many weeks later I asked Dr. Ravalli, "Did he really call you 'babe?'"

"Yes," Dr. Ravalli confessed.

"Is it short for 'Beppe' or something?"

"No, it's just what he calls me."

"Why?" I asked.

Dr. Ravalli shook his head, baffled by the mysteries of American slang and the English language. "I don't know," he said. "I really don't know."

Sept. 22, 4:28 p.m.

Oh my gosh, friends, what you've missed! You might think our days in the hospital are tranquil and lacking in incident but you would be so wrong.

Yesterday was a discouraging day: bad fever in the night and dramatic shortness of breath during the day. I was bummed. But it also provided great entertainment. There was the Fellow Smackdown: when the Pulmonology Fellow left the room to get a portable CT scan cart and returned to find his space at Rick's side occupied by the Infectious Diseases Fellow. They both puffed up their chests and exchanged ranks: "I'm Pulmonology." "I'm ID." ID won, I think because he was leading rounds later that afternoon and was going to use R. for an exhibit. Fortunately I missed that.

Then there was a far more civilized exchange later on when a Very Senior Specialist arrived with a team. This was an elder statesman who spoke directly to Rick and to me, and his school of pilot fish stayed mute, which is the way I like them. Then at the door I spied our Beloved Cardiologist, who entered beaming. He and Senior Specialist knew each other: they exchanged a nod and a handshake, and I had the sense of many words Not Being Spoken. I swear, and witnesses back me up, that Specialist said to Cardio, "Hi, babe," which was very odd between two 60-plus men. But it was like watching two Mafia dons meeting at a niece's wedding, conveying affectionate respect for each other.

And this morning, Rick actually walked down the hall without supplemental oxygen. (It trailed behind in its green tank, unused.) This, my dears, is immense. The normal amount of oxygen in "room air" is 21%, and from it our healthy lungs extract enough of the important stuff to bring the saturation in our blood to a robust, say, 95% or more. Take a breath. Think about that. Last week Rick was getting forced oxygen at 60% and his saturation rate dipped into the 80s sometimes. So we hit a milestone today.

Yet—lest the mystery aspect of the tale peter out into nothing at all, I present to you: the rash. It appeared this morning. All over his body, except for his face. I think this should be catnip to ID, but it may also bring in another specialist, because surely Dermatology wants in on this party, right? Oh, wait, newsflash from CPMC: Derm says reaction to Nexium. Seems kind of dull to me.

Rick is still too weak for visitors. He had two yesterday and they almost did him in. He just doesn't have the stamina yet to keep a social ball in the air, and you know how important that is to him.

Also, I think we can be sure the prayers are working because the medical community in all its complex glory appears still to be flying blind. So don't stop now.

Lots of love from both of us, Carol

CHAPTER ELEVEN

Hospital, Day 11

I wasn't up to reading Carol's e-mails but I know she had made a point of letting people know that visitors were still discouraged. When she was there two arrived at the same time, strangers to each other: Albert, an eighty-something neighbor of ours, and Edgar, a dapper ninety-five-year-old fellow worshipper. Originally from Barbados, Edgar's been a member of our church since the mid-'60s. When our boys were growing up, he was like a grandfather to them, always ready for high fives at coffee hour.

Edgar knows the whole hymnal by heart, and a couple of months earlier, when a bout of pneumonia landed him in the hospital, I'd gone to visit him on a Sunday afternoon, and we'd sung a few hymns together, savoring the sweetness of the music and the memory of worship, bringing church into the ward. But I couldn't sing now, not a note. I couldn't get enough breath to sustain a phrase.

Edgar sat in a chair opposite me, and then Albert came in and sat in another chair next to him. I could imagine making some sort of introduction: "Edgar, this is Albert. He teaches math at a college. In years that most devote to the leisure of retirement, he teaches a couple classes." "Albert, this is our friend Edgar, a pillar of our church. He used to work for Horn & Hardart, the old automat. Remember that?"

They sat in silence, and I sat in silence. I closed my eyes and opened them. They were still there. "This is a kind thing they are doing," I could tell myself. This was prayer in action. Accept it, enjoy it, appreciate it. But I was chagrined, embarrassed. I couldn't be the Rick Hamlin I wanted to be, the gregarious person I once was, the extrovert in action.

A friend who does pastoral care on the oncology ward of the same hospital described to me what I was going through. "Rick Hamlin had left the room. Someone else was in bed." I wanted to call that person an impostor, but that person was me as much as I am me.

Is this why tribulation is supposed to be such a good teacher? We have lost one self and haven't gained a new self yet. We are wandering in the desert. We are like Nicodemus, visiting Jesus in the middle of the night, under the cover of darkness, afraid of being seen. And what does Jesus tell us? That we need to be born anew, born of the spirit. We can't do that until we let go of that old self.

I could look out the window and see the building where a good friend had his office, a psychiatrist who runs a program at Columbia University. I could have e-mailed him and told him where I was. "Hey, Robert, guess where I am? Guess what I can see out my window? Guess who is the patient on the sixth floor being visited by every specialist you know and don't know on the Columbia-Presbyterian staff so they can check out his mystery ailment and be the one with the right answer?" Robert's a doctor. Of all people, he would understand my situation.

But I never e-mailed him.

I like to think I'm comfortable with vulnerability, my own vulnerability. I don't have a tough-guy persona. I'm not a stiff-upper-lip type. I thrive on compassion—or so I say—but maybe that's because I don't want to be the patient, don't want to be the recipient of such compassion. I want to be in charge. I want to set the scene and stage for vulnerability, control it, manage it, present it. I can be honest about all sorts of faults when I'm the writer, but then I'm putting all the bread crumbs out, dropping them in a line that will lead to the conclusion I have chosen. I wasn't in charge in a hospital bed.

My visitors left. I said good-bye to them, and they said good-bye to me. I picked up my Kindle to find a Bible quote, scrolling through verses. It would have been easier to search for it on my laptop. "All who want to save their lives will lose them. But all who lose their lives because of me will save them."

Is it possible that you have to be Nicodemus more than once in your life? You have to sneak out in the dark to listen for wisdom that you thought you already knew. You were the wise man, the rabbi, the Pharisee, but then along comes some greater wisdom, and at least you have the wisdom to recognize it even if you're not ready to welcome it in the full light of day. You can only take this halfway step to sit at the feet of the man who is lit by the glow of his own greater knowledge.

This is the scarier part of being in the hospital, not the body-dying part but the soul-struggling part, letting go of the old you, waiting for some new you that doesn't seem like it could ever find you in this place of drugs, tests, beeping monitors, meals on trays, experts coming and going. You need to be born from above, born anew, born when you thought you were going to die.

Would I ever sing again? Maybe that was one of those things I would have to give up, losing that part of myself. Perhaps I needed to mourn that, all those moments of song. I could find them on my phone, recorded not so long ago. I could log on to Facebook and see them, listen to them, remembering who I once was.

God has given me a lifeline in music, opening me up, straightening me out, making the rough places plain, quieting my soul even as I make noise. Not for nothing does singing the blues put me in the pink. Even sad songs can make sadness bearable, putting thoughts into words and music. A song is a way to remember a text, the brain holding on to what's glued to it by rhythm and tune. Surely the ancient poets chanted the verses of their epic poems because it was easier to remember them that way.

I still find myself humming a high-speed version of the A-B-C song just to be sure that W comes after U and V. Short and long passages of Scripture are only retrievable because someone set them to music. "O clap your hands, all ye people. Shout unto God with the voice of triumph," I sing to myself, with thanks to Ralph Vaughan Williams, who gave me the tune. "The Lord's my shepherd, I'll not want," is set in my head to a melody called "Brother James's Air." Jesus might have said, "I am the bread of life," but the moment I see those words I start humming a hymn that doesn't always scan but always brings us to our feet at church.

In honor of turning sixty I posted a song a day for sixty days on Facebook, videos I took on my phone. I didn't overthink it, for better or for worse. A colleague at the office wanted me to hold off for a week or two, just to do more promotion. I was more afraid that if I didn't jump in—jumping in the deep end—I would never do it. I began on a Friday in May, without any list. "In honor of my sixtieth birthday this year I'm singing sixty songs in sixty days. Here's the first one."

At once I was committed. A promise is a promise. Sixty might prove to be a bigger number than I thought, perhaps a reminder that living for sixty years was longer than I remembered.

The first song, "Precious Lord," I recorded near my office on Fulton Street, with the Freedom Tower in the background—would people notice? I did two takes and that was it. I planned to record each song in a different spot in the city, giving them different settings. It would become a sort of tour of my life. If Gene Kelly and Frank Sinatra could sing "New York, New York, it's a wonderful town" all over the city, couldn't I? It's not like I was shy about singing in public. I'd embarrassed my children enough over the years by breaking out in song in unexpected places.

I remember once being on the A train, heading for work, and hearing an Afro-Caribbean woman singing "Holy, Holy, Holy" as she made her way down the car. She might have been passing out tracts too—I have a soft spot for anyone handing out tracts—but her intention was in the music: "Lord, God, Almighty, early in the morning our song shall rise to Thee." I knew the words well but I didn't recognize the tune. Was it something from the islands?

"How does that go?" I asked her. "Holy, holy, holy" she resumed, and I sang along. To the amusement or irritation of the other commuters? I don't really know. We were having fun with our music. "Do you know this version?" I asked, singing a few bars, and then I had to get off at my stop, not without getting blessed by her, which was as sweet as any song we might have sung.

Subway tunnels are good for singing, but I soon discovered how noisy New York is, the din of traffic and air conditioners and jets overhead competing with my music. It was fun to record "Moon River" outside of Tiffany's in honor of Audrey Hepburn, but the passing buses gave me a lot of competition. Same problem with "Give My Regards to Broadway" on the corner of Forty-Second and Broadway.

My repertoire is dated. I would be hard-pressed to pull up a tune written in the new millennium. I know vintage Broadway from singing along to stacks of original cast albums; I've absorbed the American Songbook through cocktail pianists and elevator Muzak; I've wallowed in hymns from the time of my birth, but any pop or rock I know was mostly picked up listening to the radio while driving the LA freeways in Mom's old Buick station wagon. My moment of would-be stardom in a rock band lasted for only one rehearsal in seventh grade, when the budding impresario realized that not only did I lack the chops and the keyboard skills, but I was clueless on the style.

That said, coming up with a song a day was easy. There are tons of them in my head. I posted first thing in the morning with something I'd recorded the previous day, never planning too far ahead lest I intimidate myself, or get so overwhelmed I'd want to give up. I was touched by the enthusiasm of friends and followers, their comments making me smile. I changed venues as often as possible but kept coming back to the subway tunnel for the acoustics, often choosing it for favorite old hymns, like "How Great Thou Art" and "Great Is Thy Faithfulness."

I came back again for "What a Friend We Have in Jesus."

I walked down to the end of the Brooklyn-bound J-Z platform. Any moment a train would be coming. You could tell from how many people were waiting. New Yorkers have a sixth sense about crowds on subway platforms. A crowded platform can be good news—"Oh, good, the train should be coming soon"—until it becomes bad news—"Oh drat, there must be some mess-up or delay, because the platform is way too crowded, and my train will probably be cramped, or I might not even get on..."

This was good news. The train rumbled in, and everybody stepped on. There was no other train to take at this platform, nothing else coming down the track. I waited for the noise of the departing subway to disappear down the tunnel, then held up my phone to record "What a friend we have in Jesus/All our sins and griefs to bear/What a privilege to carry/Everything to God in prayer..." (Best comment came from a Birmingham, Alabama, friend who said she couldn't quite recognize the lyrics without their usual Southern twang.) I botched it once and then tried again.

I was halfway through this second take—or maybe it was the third—when I heard someone whistling. The platform was filling up. The next train would be coming. *That guy whistling is really going to ruin this take. I'm going to have to do it all over again*, I told myself. Then I listened a little more closely. He was whistling with me. He was whistling the tune, "Have we trials and temptations/Is there trouble anywhere...?" My partner in crime, my partner in harmony, he was right there with me.

I still messed up a lyric in one place, but this one was too good to redo. I finished up and called out on the platform, "Who was whistling?" I looked both ways. A guy in a yellowish shirt waved his hand at the far front end.

"Thanks," I said. "That was terrific."

When I watched the video I could see him, in his yellowish shirt, walking right behind me to his spot on the platform where he began tuning in.

It made me happy. The whole thing made me happy, all my griefs to bear, a way out of trouble anywhere.

I found a new use for my phone in the hospital. I began taking photos of all my caregivers: the doctors, the nurses, the techs, the janitors, the woman who brought my meals.

"I'm not going to post this picture," I said. "I just want it for me."

There was Infectious Diseases, with his stethoscope looped over the back of his neck, and the night nurse, with two name tags, and my beloved Jay with "RN" in red letters on his white shirt, and the Chinese nurse at the nurses' station who didn't want to have her photo taken at all. She distrusted the whole project. The bearded PT is wearing plastic gloves and green surgicals in my photo. We'd just come back from a walk. "I need to get a picture of your colleague," I told him, "the one who walked with me for the first time." Had she met and found the man of her dreams in the few days since we'd last talked?

Dermatology is wearing a regimental tie, the food lady has a black sweater and a sweet smile. I have two shots of The Attending in her white coat, her hands flying as she talks. Earnest and tireless, she saw me twice a day, even on weekends. You can see the clock on the wall behind the chatty intern who visited me almost every day; it says four thirty. The resident, with his hipster beard, is giving me the thumbs-up. All these shots are taken from the patient's point of view. They remind me of the photos four-year-old Tim took with a throwaway camera when he was lying in traction for twenty-six days, trapped in bed but looking up at one friend or caregiver after another, a healing brigade pasted in a scrapbook. This would be my record, my gallery.

There was the woman in pulmonology who reminded me of a travel agent, and the nurse from San Diego whose father was a cardiologist. She has the clearest of blue eyes and the whitest of blonde hair. She came to New York to study nursing because all she wanted in life was to be a nurse at a big hospital like Presbyterian, and here she is.

When the nurse's assistant came in to take my vitals I asked, "Will you let me take your picture?"

"Why?"

"So I can remember the people who helped me."

"You've got to let me fix my hair and makeup first." *Did she blush?*

She came back a few hours later. Frankly I couldn't detect a shade of difference, but she did a shimmying dance for my camera. The janitor came by, collecting trash, and I took his picture, to his surprise. "These aren't for Facebook or Instagram," I said. "They're just for me."

Like I said, I had always promised myself when Timothy was in the hospital that we would go back and thank the staff. We never did. Once you're out and well you don't want to go back. Ever. I was wiser this time. I wouldn't come back to 6 Garden North and South willingly. But I would carry the people with me the way I carried songs with me. Not just in my head but in my phone.

September 24, 9:24 p.m.

New idea here. I'm thinking that maybe framing Rick's illness as linear narrative was a mistake. Events seem to be too loose and baggy for that. Here's what popped into my head yesterday after a deeply annoying snafu: Rick and I are on the Elderhostel trip nobody wants to take.

Just imagine the listings in that catalog and you can see the qualities in this offering that would drive people away:

1/duration. Way too long. We're heading toward two weeks in the hospital, during which we could have bicycled all over Iceland, I imagine.

2/cost. Nuff said.

3/food. Actually, Rick eats some of it, to keep his strength up. Ew.

4/surroungings. I understand Elderhostels are sometimes rustic, but institutional medical architecture circa 1982...No.

Remember the rash? It got itchy! All over his body, all night long! Dermatology did show up, bringing our roster of medical disciplines to six. He fasted all night Tuesday prior to having a TEE (sonogram, esophagus, better picture of heart; Cardio ordered it) and they screwed up so he didn't have it after 12 hours hungry and thirsty. However he was just taken downstairs for it this morning. Had a CT scan of his abdomen (looking for enlarged lymph nodes) at 1:00 a.m. Possibly looking for TB, for which there is no blood test. Which I didn't know. So that was an educational nugget.

Good news is more walking all over the floor, without oxygen, and I believe no fever yesterday. He's getting better, though still a long way from well. So still no visitors and we're still not answering phones. As ever, feel free to forward this to other concerned friends.

Lots of love to all of you from the whole Hamlin family. If we didn't feel your support and prayers, this episode would be no joking matter.

CHAPTER TWELVE

Hospital, Days 12 and 13

I was right. My inner voice had spoken the truth. I was going to get out of the hospital. It was going to happen. I didn't know when, but soon. I still had a rash, which baffled the doctors—Dermatology was my newest friend. I was incredibly weak, skinnier than I'd ever been, down to 133 pounds. I looked sepulchral in the bathroom mirror, my cheeks sunken, dark circles beneath my eyes. But at least I was able to go to the bathroom by myself, no bedpans, no buzzing for a nurse. I didn't have an IV attached to me twenty-four hours a day. They'd taken me off the regular heart monitor. I didn't need supplementary oxygen anymore. The maddening fevers were diminishing. Still no diagnosis, but did I need a diagnosis if I was getting better? Couldn't I be that mystery patient who was sick and then got better?

Jesus said with faith we can move mountains. "I assure you that whoever says to this mountain, 'Be lifted up and thrown into the sea'—and doesn't waver but believes that what is said will really happen—it will happen. Therefore I say to you, whatever you pray and ask for, believe that you will receive it, and it will be so for you." That's the sort of faith I can never find for myself, but now it occurred to me: It isn't something you do for yourself. It's a gift you're given, God's grace.

Glenn appeared at the hospital one of those last days. Glenn is an old college friend. We'd sung a cappella together on campus. He still lives in New Jersey and drove in to see me. "I can't believe you came all this way," I said.

Glenn is a musician, a poet, and a computer entrepreneur. He's also a prayer person. "Mom's praying for you," he said. "And Aunt Myra." Aunt Myra was a longtime *Guideposts* reader.

The sun was setting, and I wanted to see it. "Let's go for a walk," I said. There was no view of the river from my room.

We walked farther on the sixth floor than I had ever walked before, leaving the safe confines of my ward and entering another. Here, you could see the Hudson River and the George Washington Bridge without any obstructions.

A barge cut through the water, pushed by a tugboat. The rush hour traffic rumbled across the bridge, slower out than in. Life was going on. I needed to reenter it. It was like taking a big breath before you dive into a cold lake on a hot day. You know you need to do it; you know you'll be glad of it. But you linger on dry land, waiting, taking more than one big breath, wondering if you're ready.

"They have a much better view here," Glenn said, "than you do on your side of the building."

"They do," I said.

He brought me a book, *Good Poems for Hard Times*, edited by Garrison Keillor. I wished Glenn had brought me one of his own poems. We sat in the lounge that faced the river, the September sunlight bathing the room. How many such beautiful days had I missed from here? How could I recover them all? I thought of Howard's infamous words, "You can't make it up."

This time wouldn't be lost forever. I was determined to make it count for something. Even doing nothing can be a blessing. "Wasting time with God," Tim calls it. Sitting with an old friend in a hospital lounge, ignoring the rash itching beneath the hospital gown, clinging to the promise of returning health, believing in healing, wanting to trust it.

There weren't many other patients there or family members.

"What is this ward for?" I asked a nurse.

"Oncology," she said.

Glenn and I looked at each other. Oncology got the better view. They needed it. But then, didn't we?

Jim showed up, another college friend and former roommate. He lives down in DC. I couldn't figure out how he managed to be at the hospital. "I had a business trip up here," he said. "And my interview this afternoon got canceled. I figured that was a sign that I was meant to come visit you."

When he worked in New York we used to have lunch once a month. In addition to talking about our jobs and families, we talked about our faith. For a buttoned-up lawyer, he has a surprising, winsome, childlike love of God and an enthusiasm for Scripture. Wherever he is, he always finds some Bible study to join. That would be like him, to see this chance to visit me as a sign.

"Your timing is a little off," I said. I was lying on a gurney, being wheeled off to another floor for another test, a transesophageal echocardiogram or a TEE, to get a better view of my heart. I didn't like the idea of them putting a tube down my esophagus, but if it helped in coming up with a diagnosis, I would do it. I would do anything. "I've got to do a test. I haven't eaten for hours. Have to do it on an empty stomach."

The aide started pushing me down the hall.

"I'll come with you," Jim said, walking fast.

It reminded me of the one time I'd visited him in his hometown of Kalamazoo, Michigan. He and his dad met me at the bus station on a cold November day. We had only a half hour before we had to head back to Princeton. "Let me show you the town," his dad said, looking at his watch. "We'll run."

And we did, jogging through the empty streets of downtown Kalamazoo on a Sunday morning to see the sights.

Jim was almost jogging now, making the most of the time we had. Life was precious, not a moment to waste. Who knew when we'd see each other again and under what circumstances? You jogged with your friend down bright halls, answering his questions about the kids, work, and Bible study.

Jim stayed with me till the last minute, until I was rolled into a cold, dimly lit room that made me think of the OR when I'd had heart surgery.

"Would you like a blanket?" they asked.

"Please." This was like the blanket they gave me in the OR right before heart surgery because I was freezing, my teeth chattering. I knew back then that they'd take it off as soon as the anesthesia took hold, as soon as they could "stretch" the sternum and saw through it, as soon as they put me on the heart-lung machine. But until then we could act as though I were an old man in winter, sitting on a park bench, needing a blanket to stay warm.

Pam came the last night I was in the hospital. Carol had left, and I'd finished dinner. It was getting dark outside and surely time for her to go home and have dinner with Jeff, her husband, but she stayed.

I wanted to know how her sons were doing.

She asked me about our boys.

I wanted to know about how her work was—she's a documentary filmmaker and her latest project sounded interesting.

She asked me if I was writing anything particular before I landed in the hospital.

I wanted to know what Jeff was doing.

She asked about Carol.

We've known each other almost forty years. Carol says she is the only one of our friends who manages to get us to talk more about ourselves than anyone else. That must be some achievement, but it says more to me about her powers of listening. We met senior year in college when she sang with the women's a cappella group at Harvard, the Radcliffe Pitches, and I sang with the Princeton Footnotes, and we had a concert together. Then she was a neighbor in Washington Heights when our boys were first born. She showed up in the middle of the night to be with William while we rushed to the hospital to await the birth of Tim.

We'd celebrated Thanksgivings together year after year.

"What if I can't do some of the things I used to be able to do?" I asked.

"Like what?"

"Running."

"In time."

"Singing."

"Can you sing now?"

I shook my head. My voice was hoarse from the TEE, that tube down my throat.

How much was I willing to bargain with God? Was I ready for some horse-trading? I had my life. I'd come closer to death than anybody would like, but I was still alive, still kicking, breathing. I would get to go home. "You've given me my life back, God, but what kind of life is it going to be?"

Recovery from heart surgery had been different from this. As soon as possible they'd had me up and walking around the ward. The physical therapist took me up and down steps even in the hospital. When I was released to go home after heart surgery the instructions were: Walk, walk, walk and walk some more. No naps. Get some exercise. It was push, push, push.

Now I had to marshal my forces, had to be careful not to go too far. It was rest, rest, rest. My stamina was gone.

"Do they know what you had?" Pam asked.

"No. They're still trying to figure that out. But I got better." My new mantra, the only way I could explain it: the doctors kept me alive, the prayers healed me.

There was a lot more spiritual healing and emotional healing that needed to happen, my psyche and soul catching up to what Western medicine had done for my body. The old me was gone. I couldn't trust my body anymore the way I once had. Would I always be second-guessing it? Would every slight cough or cold, would the smallest fever scare me into thinking that I was going to land in the hospital again, unable to breathe?

I didn't want to live in fear. I would have to keep working on my faith, dig deeper, love more, trust more, let go more. All of it would have to come by the grace of God because the doing wasn't going to do it.

Pam left. I was alone in the night, the breathing of my hospital roommate coming through the curtain. I had to wait for the night nurse to check me out one last time and then I could sleep—attempt to sleep, really, because I never slept well in the hospital.

The old Rick Hamlin was gone. The new Rick had to be rejiggered and remade. Re-hatched. "Born from above," as the Bible puts it.

With Carol's help I crafted a letter to the staff, and she printed it up so the head nurse would have a copy in her files. "To the staff at 6 Garden North…

"In the nearly two weeks that I was a patient I was continually touched by your passion for your work. Whether you were cleaning the floors (bravo, Peter) or taking someone's vitals or listening for a heartbeat, a job was never sloppily or casually done."

This would be a way to move forward, living with gratitude, gratitude every minute.

"You were great at listening to questions, answering them whenever possible, getting more information if necessary. You rely on machines because they are necessary, but never did I feel that someone was looking over my head at my 'numbers' rather than at me, the person in the bed."

I didn't want it to sound fawning, but authentic, from the heart. Someone once told me that the most important thing to put in any thank-you note were details, so that you didn't sound vague. Easy enough in this case.

"You also seem to like each other and respect each other. I liked hearing you greet each other and laugh with each other. When people like each other, you like being with them. That creates a healing environment."

Maybe that's why I felt so lonely at night. I didn't get

to hear other voices, didn't get that sense that life was still moving forward. It was just me in my hospital bed.

"You work for a huge organization, but to my amazement, I didn't feel like a cog in a wheel, a paper that needs to be moved around from desk to desk. This must take enormous work on your behalf, because there is surely much paperwork that must be done. But you made me feel that I was a person, not a number.

"You have many patients to care for. I am grateful that I was one of them. I hope I don't ever have to come back as a patient again, but if I do, I would be grateful to be among you again."

OK, that last line wasn't completely accurate. I wouldn't EVER want to be a patient. Never again.

Sept. 25, 6:56 p.m.

And then, poof! We're home. Just like that. Well, there was a glitch, of course, not just the usual paperwork but at the last minute we were held up a couple of hours because Rick needed to be given a last-ditch set of pills for scabies, of all things, which someone on the floor has. Scabies, which in animals is called "mange." Lest he come from the hospital mangy.

We spent some time this morning with the extraordinary attending doctor who was in overall charge, trying to formulate just what this was. Here's what she came up with:

"Respiratory failure and severe systemic inflammation caused by idiopathic infection." I.e., Rick got really really sick and nobody knows why. We did add one more specialty to our roster of the medical disciplines when an allergist came in this morning to discuss The Rash and its possible antecedents, but she was such a late entrant and the symptom was so comparatively minor that she didn't have a chance of ownership. Rick will follow up with pulmonology and his internist.

He went around the floor this last couple of days taking pictures of the people who have taken care of him. They were thrilled—this was clearly a novelty. And we have now a little album of smiling faces. We grew very, very fond of these people: docs, cleaners, aides, nurses, therapists, med students. If you need to be gravely ill, try to get onto 6 Garden North at Columbia-Presbyterian.

Your own smiling faces, your thoughts, your prayers, your food and your cards and your chocolate and well-wishes and flowers have all kept us afloat. And you praying people can now slip in one more prayer—of thanksgiving. We don't expect much in the way of long-term issues, though the worriers among us will be sure to keep that eventuality covered.

Rick can now communicate directly, so go to it, folks, I'm bowing out. But not without one additional story.

A nursing student friend of ours came to see us when Rick was still in the step-down unit on heavy-duty oxygen. She figured out very quickly, she said, that he was the favorite on the floor. So much so that when she left the room, one of the younger nurses asked, "Is he famous?" And she said firmly, "Yes."

We've spent a lot of time in the last two weeks with people who were not as supported as we were. So at the end of this two weeks, here's how we feel:

Lucky.

Much love,

Carol

CHAPTER THIRTEEN

Home

W rite about Italy." That was my prescription. "Remember your experience in Italy. Recall the time. Recover it, immerse yourself in it, dream about it, see it again. Remember the people and the place. Put the words down."

I was home, but with very little energy. Stamina had gone out the window. I didn't know if I'd ever get it back. There was no possibility of putting myself on the subway train and dragging myself into the office, as much as I would have liked that, as much as I yearned to see my colleagues, to sit at my desk, to attack a manuscript that needed fixing, to interview a story subject, to gab in the kitchen with another editor. That would have to wait.

I felt guilty about being home, but bless my dear colleagues, they preempted me and reminded me that I was on sick leave and that I was absolutely not to consider coming in. In e-mails they insisted that I was not to *think* about work until I was really well. I knew I was being read the riot act: "You are Absolutely Forbidden to come to the office until you are so well that there will be no risk of any relapses, Hamlin. Don't push it. Stay put."

What was I to do instead?

First thing in the morning, after sitting in silence for half an hour, after brushing the cat, after cooking myself a bowl of oatmeal and eating it over the opened pages of the *New York Times*, I opened my laptop, sat on Carol's big yellow exercise ball at the dining room table, and wrote about Italy. I was on assignment. I might say that my muse had put me up to it, but really, it was a God thing, a divine command.

I felt rotten. My body still ached. My breathing wasn't up to par. And I was so tired, too tired to concentrate for long on a book. Even Tolkien would have put me to sleep. But I could write and, oddly enough, the writing took me out of myself. It released me from second-guessing about where the aches were coming from and wondering what they meant and fearing that I was plunging down mortality's rabbit hole again.

Italy was the perfect subject. I was once again the twenty-two-year-old kid who landed in London—it was cheap—and took the ferry across the English Channel, heading toward the Continent, imagining I was a modern J. M. W. Turner, tying himself to a mast in the midst of turbulent seas to experience a storm up close—though there was no storm that October day. From France I took a train down to the Italian peninsula, changing trains in Milan and getting into a car that was marked FIRENZE, Florence my final destination. I savored the views: the golden hills of Tuscany framed by gray cypress, dotted with dark green olive trees, crisscrossed with vines, the fruit getting heavy, ready for the harvest.

The landscape hadn't changed in hundreds of years; it

looked like the background of some cinquecento portrait of a saint or Jesus sitting on his mother's lap. My guidebook described "the diaphanous light," and even if I didn't know what the word meant, I understood it. God was shading the hills with his own celestial paintbrush.

I didn't know a soul in Florence, had no practical prospects at all, had no idea what I was going to do, but in a matter of days I found friends and a place to live, a church where I could worship and a choir to sing in, and a job as a teacher of English as a foreign language. I ended up staying for two years, singing, teaching, supporting myself, becoming someone new, starting out from scratch on my own.

I began to see the wisdom of this "only-for-me" writing assignment. I was being taken back to a time when I was born anew, forging a new identity as I would have to forge one now. Back then I didn't know enough to be scared, to know how harebrained my "I want to live in Italy" notion was. I just did it, drawing on hidden resources and the grace of God.

Fear was the enemy now, worse than any bodily fatigue. I was glad to be back in my own bed, glad to have Carol next to me, glad to gaze out the bedroom window to the Hudson River and the Palisades beyond, but this spot, this sanctuary, was the very place I had become mortally ill, my temperature rising, the "idiopathic infection" taking hold of me and shattering my self-assured view that death was a long way off. I had been in this bed when my breathing got worse and worse, and my temperature soared until I went off to the ER. I would wake up now in the middle of the night and look at myself just to see if I was still alive, my soul checking on my loud beating heart. I knew without asking that Carol was doing the same thing: looking at me in the middle of the night to see if I was breathing. Was I still here?

I have a friend from church whose husband, after a losing battle with depression, took his own life in their apartment. As she was waiting for the police to finish their inquiry and waiting for the ambulance to take the body, she invited friends to sit with her in the living room. She is a musician, a wonderful singer, and as stunned and numb as she was from her devastating loss, she started singing hymns and they joined her, claiming faith in the midst of sorrow. In the weeks and months that followed she had to teach herself to see her home as the sanctuary it had always been and not the scene of tragedy. She even invited a priest to bless the home, like Jesus driving a demon out of a possessed soul.

Fear was my demon, and I would do all I could to drive it out, reclaiming the places of my life. Morning after morning I would sit at my laptop at the dining room table and remember what it was to be reborn, to start from scratch. It had happened more than once in my life. It would happen again.

All those friends who had prayed for us, now they showed their love in an even more tangible fashion. They brought us food. For weeks we did not have to cook a meal or even go to the store to buy lunch and dinner. Food simply appeared at our door.

Word had gone out through our congregation, our apartment complex, our network of friends. FreshDirect or Blue Apron boxes arrived just when we wondered if we should heat up the Tupperware leftovers from someone else's generosity that was still in the fridge. Someone would call and say they were coming with mac and cheese or a roast or a pizza, and then also bring soup and sandwiches and some homemade brownies and a bottle of wine. Whenever possible I was glad to sit and talk, but nobody stayed for dinner. We were on our own, and that was good.

My younger sister, Diane, flew out just as I was coming home, and her presence was a blessing, another adult, another pair of hands, someone else who could wash the dishes or do the laundry, jobs I normally never minded doing. But now just to take the trash down two floors to the basement left me winded. No way could I come back up without pausing on the landing halfway there. Would I ever climb those stairs again without running out of breath?

We were flooded with cards and gifts, flowers, books, boxes of chocolate, more wine. I lingered over each card, reading the words to myself, the good wishes the prayers. "One more person who prayed for me," I would think. It was humbling and touching and also embarrassing.

I couldn't take it in, all that kindness, all that warmth and affection and generosity. It was too much.

Invariably I wrote back, sending e-mails or mailing a postcard or note, and then—this sounds so callous and ungracious—I would throw the card away. I'm not sure what the issue was. Was I trying to get myself out of Sick Land? Was I tired of being the patient? Was I ashamed of being vulnerable? Mostly I felt too indebted. I was being given more than I could ever return. I was being told in a million ways how loved and cherished I was, and I couldn't take it.

One day, after going through a stack of cards, sending off e-mails to the givers, I took them to the kitchen wastebasket and paused. *Don't*, I simply told myself. *Rick, keep these. Keep all of them. Not forever. But for now. Receive the love, Rick. It is as rich and unearned and satisfying as God's own love.*

This was who the new Rick was supposed to be. This was how I would be born anew. By knowing that I was loved, incredibly, impossibly, unimaginably, from above and beyond, and from close by in dozens of ways. The stack of cards and notes was to build and build until I could somehow hold the message, the hardest one for me to take in, probably because it would mean letting go of my ego and accepting that who I am is not the result of all my tireless good work and charm. I said it at the beginning of this memoir: "It's not what you do, it's what God does. It's not how hard you try, it's how willing you are not to try."

Believe it, Hamlin. PRAY IT. Take it in.

I began a long series of return visits to my various doctors down at the hospital so they could check on my progress.

The first visit was with my pulmonologist, Dr. DiMango. It was only the first week after I'd been released from the hospital, and Carol and I took the bus down to her office. She was incredibly thorough, as always. We sat with her for a good hour as she logged on to the computer and looked through all of my tests. She turned back to us and gave us the only theory we've gotten of what might have caused this disastrous infection.

"I think you had an allergic reaction to the sulfa drugs you were given."

"The sulfa drugs."

"Yes, what they gave you for the boil on the back of your leg."

"Could I get that sick from an allergic reaction?" I asked.

"Yes," she said, "if it goes unaddressed. It's just a very good thing that you went to the Emergency Room as soon as you did."

One thing we did right.

We thanked her. A couple of weeks later I came back for some tests on my lungs and my breathing. This time I came by myself. "You can always tell they're doing better," she said, "when they come without their spouse."

I laughed.

I saw the Beloved Cardiologist and the Wise Internist, Seth, greeting his office staff with joy. I took their pictures to add to the gallery of caregivers on my phone, although I did not bring back the Columbia-Presbyterian sweatshirt Seth had given me that day I was in his office, shivering from fever.

On all these trips I had a foreboding sense whenever I looked up to the sixth floor of Garden North, my home for those two agonizing weeks. For years this corner of Washington Heights had seemed like sacred ground because it was where our children had been born. I would never forget the joy I'd felt walking that fifteen-block stretch from our hospital to our apartment, filled with the wonder of their births. No more. Newer memories crowded out those happy days. I glanced up at the skyway over Fort Washington Avenue that leads to Garden North, and could remember being pushed down its corridor at 2:00 a.m. on my way to the ICU step-down unit, that night when my health seemed at its most perilous. Instead of thinking with gratitude, "Gosh, this is the place where I got better," I recalled those terrifying moments of hopelessness. My body remembered what my mind wanted to forget, my bones knowing their own mortality like Jesus foreseeing what was ahead. If only I could remake this domain. That was a challenge of being truly healed.

One sunny fall day I was coming back from a test at the sprawling medical campus—another look at my clearing lungs—and that day I had enough strength to walk those fifteen blocks instead of taking a cab or a bus, so I paused in a park along the way, sitting on a bench in an urban sliver of green. Basking in the sun, I gazed at a surfboard of native schist rising out of the grass. I remembered how these benches used to be full of the old German-Jewish residents, refugees from World War II who lived here when we'd first moved to the neighborhood. Most of them had long since died or moved to Florida, but they were the ones who'd welcomed us when we first came here. Our lovely next-door neighbor Hildegard, who had escaped from Frankfurt, wryly claimed, "You're refugees from the Upper West Side." I suppose we were.

Now I was the gray-haired man sitting on a park bench, watching kids running up and down the dark whale's back of schist, jumping from it, laughing like our kids used to. This was our Promised Land back when they were young, our Canaan, the place we had claimed as our own, the place that sustained us and made us happy. I felt I needed to claim it all over again. I would not let new fears rob me of the joys of the past or the joys to be found on a glorious fall day.

"These fifteen blocks are still sacred to me, Lord. You are still here as you were here in the middle of winter, when the snow was melting and Will was born and Tim was born. You are here now."

This was the spiritual work of recovery.

After I finished my morning sessions of writing about Italy, I would venture out and walk—ever so slowly at first—to the park up to the north of us, Fort Tryon Park, where I normally ran when I was well. No running now.

No running yet. *But enjoy the day, Rick. Be grateful. Be glad. You are loved. You are unconditionally loved by the Greatest Lover in the universe.* Love so amazing, so divine, as the hymnist put it, demands my soul, my life, my all.

I wanted to recover my singing voice too. I gave myself a musical project. Just as I had sung a song a day for sixty days to celebrate turning sixty, I would sing a song a day for Advent and post them online. Alisa, a pianist and composer, recommended a couple of songs that we could record together. I downloaded the music and put myself at the keyboard, learning the notes, doing it when Carol was out of the house because I didn't want her to hear my scratchy-sounding tones.

It was hard at first to find the right register to sing in, the places where my voice felt comfortable. The old mix of head voice and chest voice was gone, a new one had to be found. I suspected that the tube they sent down my esophagus for that last big test in the hospital, the TEE, had done something to the vocal cords. But I was determined to get my voice back.

Learning a new piece of music, memorizing lyrics, getting the intervals, was another source of healing. "Emmanuel," I sang, "our God is with us. And if God is with us, who can stand against us..." Sustaining the notes started to come easier, finding the breath, making music again. My stamina still had a long way to go, but singing was coming back. I could make music again. At least for myself.

I returned to work. On my first day there I took a

picture of myself at my desk, my cheeks still a bit drawn, and posted it on Facebook, letting everybody know the good news. I was back in the office. The picture got plenty of comments and kind wishes, but what amused me most—this will show you how small-minded I can be— was that though it was well received, it got a lot less traffic than that first post I did in the hospital, alerting people to my dangerous illness. Note to self: bad news gets more hits than good news. No journalistic surprise there.

I was so glad to see my colleagues, grateful for their prayers, grateful for all the work they had done covering for me in my absence. We're a small editorial team putting together the magazine, and with a zillion deadlines every month the work can't just take a pause and come to a rest. On it goes. Once again I had that sense of indebtedness. No way could I pay everybody back. *Accept it, Rick,* I told myself. *Receive it. Be grateful.* Gratitude was the only way I could pay it back.

"Welcome back," my colleague Kelly said that first happy but tiring day when a half day was more than enough. "If I find you still here at five after three, you're fired!" she said.

I took some secret pleasure in knowing that I had anticipated a couple of deadlines, and that in my absence my colleagues had logged on to my computer and found two short articles that were due when I was in the hospital. I would have done more work on them, but heck, I was glad they could be used.

I returned to church, but it was a while before I had the energy to return to choir. I wanted, though, as soon as possible, to visit Wesley, the homebound ninety-four-year-old Tuskegee Airman and consummate musician who had been a member of our church. I wanted to be sure I was well enough that I wouldn't pass along any germs to him.

On a Sunday afternoon I took the subway up to his place in the Bronx. He looked weaker and thinner, his voice softer. He winced in pain when I touched his shoulders in the hospital bed. His best friend from World War II, his best buddy, had died since I'd seen him last, and he felt the loss, but we sang again together, Wesley making harmony with whatever I picked out of the hymnal. He would not be long in this world.

"I'm sorry that I was away for so long," I told him. "I was sick and in the hospital."

"I know," he said. "I prayed for you."

I saw him a couple more times; each time he was weaker. He went into the hospital, came home, and was on hospice care. One day in the middle of the week I got a call from a fellow parishioner, "Can you come visit Wesley? I don't think he'll be around much longer."

"I can't come up right now," I said, "but I'll be there this weekend."

I hung up the phone, and then had second thoughts. What if he didn't make it to Saturday?

I called right back. "Let me sing to Wesley now," I said

to his caregiver who answered the phone. "I'll sing one of the hymns he liked. If you can hold the phone up to his ear, I'm sure he'll hear it." They say that hearing is one of the last of our senses to go.

I darted into a conference room at the office and closed the door and sang "Amazing Grace" into the phone. It was around 1:00 in the afternoon. "God bless you, Wesley," I said, promising to call back later with another song, another hymn.

That afternoon at around 5:00 I was in Times Square on my way to an appointment and I picked up my phone. This time I wanted to sing "Be Thou My Vision," another one of his favorites. I dialed, got his caregiver, identified myself, and asked if I could sing for Wesley. Could she hold up the phone for him to hear?

"He passed," she said, tears in her voice.

"He died?"

"Just this afternoon, shortly after you called."

"I'm so sorry," I said. "Thank you for caring for him. Thank you," I said, not sure I could say anything else.

I stood in the street and sang the words to myself, to anyone who was passing me in Times Square. It was that last verse I wanted to sing for him. "High King of Heaven, my victory won/May I reach Heaven's joys, O bright Heav'n's Sun!/Heart of my own heart, whate'er befall,/ Still be my Vision, O Ruler of all."

His victory was won.

Healing

Y ou want something different, you want change. You don't want to live in fear. You can't just banish the dark thoughts with a snap of your fingers. You want to be bathed in light inside and out, basking in its glow. You give yourself the daily discipline—the delight—of sitting on the sofa with your eyes closed, connecting to God above as much as the God within. You listen to your heart beating, keeping count as you keep count of your days. The busyness of your life catches up to you at the very moment when you want to forget all the busyness. You become anxious at this very time when you're doing battle with all anxieties.

You are sitting here to let it all go and yet you're holding on to the nattering self-talk. Letting go alone won't work. You have to give it up. "You take it," you say to the divine. "Take all this garbage and do something with it. Transform it the way you turn our compost into mulch." You, the praying person, put yourself in a one-way tug-of-war with God, wishing he would win and leave you lying in the grass without a rope to hold, not even the hard knot of your thoughts.

You could say to your more secular friends that this is meditation, which is a notion that seems to be acceptable in multiple circles, from Hollywood screenwriters who haul themselves off to Indian ashrams to the ranks of engineers in Silicon Valley who have been taught that meditation is a boost to their creativity, a way to increase their company's net worth. But this meditation—this prayer time—is pure Resurrection thinking. You're claiming new life. You've made yourself a Jesus follower, for better or for worse, and like the disciples, you know that your faith doesn't mean squat without the Resurrection. You are praying to a God who became a man and knows what you're going through because he went through it all and ten times worse; then he died and rose from the dead, changing everything.

Like the disciples, you have trouble at times believing. You don't always recognize him—this Resurrected One—in your midst. You could be on the road to Emmaus, listening to him, walking with him, entranced by his words, but you don't know him until he breaks bread with you, and then he simply vanishes before your sight, a phantom of your thoughts. You didn't even have a chance to embrace him. Even if you were like Mary Magdalene in the garden, taking in the empty tomb, you didn't recognize your savior, the one you loved, until he said your name.

You had it all wrong. He is your teacher and friend and source of transformation. That's who you're addressing as you sit here in the silence, the garbage truck outside cranking up its mechanical arm, dumping the trash into its middle, swallowing it up, as you dump your trash into God's pit.

It's not as though you expect a clean slate. Even when your sixth-grade teacher wiped the chalkboard clear there were hints of the equations and vocabulary words left there, the pentimento of previous lessons and teachers. "Rabbi," Mary called him. "Teacher." She knew him when he called her by name.

We flew to South Africa for Easter week, flew there to be with Tim. We don't normally get travel insurance on flights. It's too expensive; it's like betting against yourself; it seems a bad omen. But we got travel insurance for this trip. It all seemed so risky. I was well, but was I well enough to take a fifteen-hour overnight flight to Johannesburg and then another shorter flight, once we got there, to Cape Town? Talk about stamina. Talk about endurance.

I went to the doctor for a checkup beforehand, just to make sure it was all right. What did he request? The usual shots for a foreign land, and that was it. Wasn't there more to be afraid of? There it was, the fear still there, the fear after all these months of recovery, rebuilding strength, running again, singing in the choir, serving on committees, having dinner with friends, writing, going to the museum, seeing movies, being New Yorkers, but wondering still if I was pushing it, doing too much too soon, doing more than I should ever do.

"We're going to South Africa to be with our son," I explained.

"You'll need to get a hepatitis shot," Seth said.

We would only make this trip for Tim.

The flight was grueling, but we got there in one piece, and soon the adrenaline of being in a new place took over.

Cape Town was gorgeous, the views from atop Table Mountain stupendous, the history of the place riveting, the visit to the cells at Robben Island where Nelson Mandela was imprisoned for eighteen years poignant. We had high tea in the colonial outpost of the Mount Nelson Hotel—the Nellie—with an Anglican priest who had done time in our parish in New York. The church is so often on the wrong side of history, but in this place, for a time, the Anglican Church was on the right side, arguing for justice, making a stand for equality. But our priest friend was still angry. He'd grown up "colored" in the crazy ghettoizing patchwork of apartheid, and even though he had good work and a good education, he spoke with bitterness about the joblessness of his twenty-seven nieces and nephews, only a third of them with work.

How long it takes for a ship to turn around even after it has turned.

We went from there to a game park to see the wild animals, going on a photo safari to take pictures of giraffes and zebras and a magnificent lion, lying improbably next to a barbed-wire fence. There was something ersatz about this game park in the Eastern Cape, and only when we got to the monastery where Tim had been living did we get a fuller story.

"It's not that old," one of the guests pointed out. "Eighteen years ago, several of the farmers in that area got together and decided to let their land go wild. They decided they'd make more money out of it as a game park than letting their wild stock graze. Also, if it were a game park, they wouldn't be obliged to house and offer jobs to the people on their farms."

The Holy Cross brothers were invited to South Africa by Archbishop Desmond Tutu shortly after the fall of apartheid, with the hope that they could be a new model for community in a country that needed to reinvent itself. They established themselves on a hilltop outside of the university city of Grahamstown, planting gardens, creating a refectory among low-lying, suburban-looking houses, building a simple sanctuary with a plate-glass window that faced due east to catch the rising sun.

We got there on Maundy Thursday, joining a half dozen other guests who were making their Holy Week retreat. We ate our meals in silence with the brothers, joining them for the offices.

Tim showed us where he lived, the rambling guesthouse where he had a room, where he Skyped his girlfriend back in America, the library with its shelves of spiritual references. We went for long walks in the sunburned hills, the terrain reminding me of central California, give or take a few baboons. We visited the school where Tim worked five days a week, opening it at six thirty in the morning, playing with the kids, working in the office, shepherding the kids when needed. This school, founded by the brothers, was for children from kindergarten through third grade, the classes taught in Xhosa, preparing them for entry into the regular state schools after that, giving them the tools they would need to succeed.

We were the lucky ones, the blessed, parents who could see the place our son had made his home and be with the people who had been his team of support these last few months. The brothers gave him the opportunity to preach on Sundays, the teachers and staff called on his skills as a writer for grant applications, the kids called him "*Bhuti* Tim," "Brother Tim," because he was their light-skinned brother for a season.

Was I like Mary Magdalene at the empty tomb, not recognizing the good news when it was already in front of me? Did I not see that this was what Resurrection could look like? A new life for Tim, a new one for me, a new one for the kids and families to whom the brothers and the school staff reached out.

Good Friday we celebrated with the brothers in the sanctuary, reliving the horrible moments of the Crucifixion, rereading the Gospel account. Parts of the service were in Afrikaans and Xhosa, the Lord's Prayer prayed in three languages at once. The congregation included neighbors who supported the brothers and their good work. And then there were some of the kids, reverencing the cross, kissing the feet of Jesus without a shred of self-consciousness. *Let the children come.*

The Easter vigil started well before dawn on Easter Day.

The brothers had broken their silence the day before to give us our parts in the liturgy, different Bible lessons to read aloud, our only light coming from the stars and the Paschal candle. There was a breeze that autumn morning, and the flame struggled to stay lit as we gathered around it in the garden. "The light of Christ," we chanted. "Thanks be to God." Three times, each time a little higher: the light of Christ, thanks be to God. We'd done this service dozens of times before back in New York, but always on the Saturday night leading into Easter. How much better it was here, on Easter Sunday, in a garden like the garden where the women came early on Easter morning, bringing spices to anoint the dead body.

The sky lightened. We moved in a procession closer to the sanctuary, neighbors joined us, the crowd clamoring for Easter, ready to claim it for themselves. Whether the brothers knew how to time it, or whether this was simply the accident of the season, the sun rose at exactly the right moment, shining into the window of the sanctuary just as we proclaimed, "Alleluia. The Lord is risen. The Lord is risen indeed."

The rest of the day, we made ourselves a feast, cooking in the refectory, the brothers pouring glasses of good South African wine, all of us chatting happily together after three days of dining in silence.

The Lord had risen indeed.

That next day, when I went for a jog across the hills, keeping my eye on the road for any poisonous snakes, lest

I accidentally step on one, I thought to myself, "The Lord is risen. The Resurrection is here. Claim it. Own it."

I had been sick, I got well. I had almost died, I was alive. I had tumbled into a fit of despair, I had found hope again. I had lost my ability to pray, I was prayed for. I was afraid, I was reassured. I had been lost, I was found. I had everything to be thankful for and to celebrate. Alleluia. I had stumbled through Calvary and landed in a verdant garden of warmth and love and happiness. Other illnesses would surely come, other dark days descend, but this I would not lose. Hold on to it. Keep it fast. The Resurrection is not something seasonal that comes around every spring. The Resurrection was once and for all. I would live it like that.

People still ask, "How are you?" "Fine, fine," I answer breezily. "You still look pretty skinny to me," they'll say. "I've always been skinny," I answer. Sometimes I wonder if it was wise to go so public about a medical disaster. Shouldn't we have kept silent about the whole thing, limiting our news to just a few close friends? I could have eased back into life as though I'd been away on sabbatical. Could have said I was on the other coast looking after family matters.

But you can't get away with such deception in this digital age of tell-all social media and viral e-mails. Besides, we needed every ounce of the support that came through them, all those prayers. I didn't read Carol's e-mails till months after I got out of the hospital, and they still startled me with their immediacy. I wanted to pray for that guy and his wife in their agonizing situation, what I'd come to term, with the levity afforded by distance, "my medical misadventure."

What I hope this remembrance does is fill in the gaps left by not-so-tell-all social media. Getting better is a lot of work; prayer is too. Recovering from a medical crisis means addressing the spin of trauma, not just sweeping it under the carpet or burying it with quick responses of "I'm fine, I'm fine." I'm grateful for the work of talk therapy, am glad I have friends with whom I can be brutally honest, despite my first instincts of sunny temper. I hope my men's group at church will tell you how boring I can be with my complaints. "There goes Rick again, talking about his slow recovery, impatient to be well."

Not long ago I was asked to preach on the passage from Romans, Paul's exhortation, "And not only that, but we also boast in our sufferings, knowing that suffering produces endurance, and endurance produces character, and character produces hope, and hope does not disappoint us, because God's love has been poured into our hearts through the Holy Spirit that has been given to us."

I had to get over my usual reaction to this passage, that it's another tiresome example of muscular Christianity, that we're supposed to stiff-upper-lip our way through life, that all our suffering produces character if we let it. Don't I know—don't you know—people for whom suffering has produced nothing but misery and more misery? This sort of transforming process Paul writes about seemed like the worst sort of wishful thinking.

The challenge of preaching about the passage was to see that it's not a matter of toughing misery out, it's not about waiting and wading through suffering in the hope that somehow, magically, it will produce this much-vaunted quality of character. As Paul goes on to point out, it's not something we do; it's something done in us and for us. It all happens because "God's love has been poured into our hearts." It's the work of the Spirit.

Which is what healing is.

I recently signed up for a seminar at our church to learn how to do healing prayer. I'd been immersing myself enough in the Gospels to see that if I wanted to really be a follower of Jesus I should be willing to do what Jesus asked, and the disciples did, to offer to heal with prayer.

I had to stifle feelings of being an impostor. Me a healer? Fat chance. But Leigh, our leader, said one thing that truly made sense to me. "It's not you who heals, it's God. When you pray for someone else to be healed, you are opening yourself up to be used by God. What it takes is surrender."

Surrender. That's pretty much where I am in prayer. Surrendering, waving a white flag in the trenches of my life, shutting down to open up, certain that the only true victories to be claimed are found in loss. I do feel healed. Sometimes fear will intrude, and a memory will startle me. Then it's time for some talk therapy and more prayer, to loosen the bonds of trauma, to shrink it down to a manageable size. Because I don't want to face fear—especially fear of death—with trembling. I yearn to be open to the truth, the whole truth, the biggest truths.

Shock comes to me when I discover a person inside me who is glad to let go, who loves life desperately and yet is equally eager to lose it, who savors this world with his whole heart and yet holds on to it with a loose grip, who knows the God within so well that the anxieties and noise outside hardly matter.

I like to think that the next time I'm hit with some medical situation that plunges me down mortality's rabbit hole I will be better prepared. I will know where I am and where I need to turn for help. But I'm not at all certain that's true. I just have to trust.

In the meanwhile, I will ask for lots of prayers. Tons of them. From anyone I've ever met and lots of people I've never known. Put me on every prayer list out there, read my name aloud in churches and synagogues, copy and paste that e-mail about me and pass it along, re-post that notice that appeared on Facebook. Thanks to all that I'm alive.

"Brothers and sisters," Paul wrote in his Second Letter to the Corinthians, "we don't want you to be unaware of the troubles that we went through in Asia. We were weighed down with a load of suffering that was so far beyond our strength that we were afraid we might not survive. It certainly seemed to us as if we had gotten the death penalty. This was so that we would have confidence in God, who raises the dead, instead of ourselves.

"God rescued us from a terrible death, and he will rescue us. We have set our hope on him that he will rescue us again since you are helping with your prayer for us."

Pray for me. I'll pray for you. It's just what we do.

About the Author

Rick Hamlin is the executive editor of *Guideposts* magazine, where he has worked for over thirty years. He is the author of three novels, the spiritual memoir *Finding God on the A Train*, and most recently *Ten Prayers You Can't Live Without*. Rick and his wife, the writer Carol Wallace, live in New York City, where they've raised their two boys. He's been a long-time contributor to the best-selling devotional *Daily Guideposts* and regularly blogs on prayer at Guideposts.org.